THE *Bounty* OF
Chester County

HERITAGE EDITION

Chester County Agricultural Development Council

THE *Bounty* OF
Chester County
HERITAGE EDITION

Published by
CHESTER COUNTY AGRICULTURAL DEVELOPMENT COUNCIL

Library of Congress Number: 00-093710
ISBN: 0-9701875-0-5

Edited, Designed, and Manufactured by
Favorite Recipes® Press
an imprint of

FRP

P.O. Box 305142, Nashville, Tennessee 37230
(800) 358-0560

Designer: Starletta Polster
Art Director: Steve Newman
Project Manager: Linda Jones

Manufactured in the United States of America
First Printing: 2001   10,000 copies

Acknowledgements

COOKBOOK COMMITTEE

Joyce E. Hershey, *Co-Chairman*

Betty A. Collins, *Co-Chairman*

Jane L. S. Davidson, *Photography, Heritage and Technical Editor*

Lynne Carroll

Trudy Dougherty

Ro Feranto

Peter Flynn

Diana Hoopes

The Cookbook Committee wishes to thank the following for their help and support:

Chester County Commissioners

    Colin A. Hanna

    Karen L. Martynick

    Andrew E. Dinniman

Agricultural Development Council

Penn State Cooperative Extension, Chester County

Chester County Family and Consumer Sciences Association

Great Valley Family and Consumer Sciences teacher, Mrs. Maryalis Bakken and her students

Chaddsford Winery

Chester County Conference and Visitors Bureau

Pat Redmond

Cover photo was photgraphed at Pete's Produce, Westtown, by George Feder Photography.

AGRICULTURAL DEVELOPMENT COUNCIL MEMBERS, 10/2000

Joyce E. Hershey, *Chair*

Tom Walsh, *Vice Chair*

Suzanne Lamborn, *Secretary*

Betty Collins

Peter Flynn

David Garrison

Furman Gyger, Jr.

Walter R. Hufford

Thomas McCaffrey

Kenneth Miller

Nancy Mohr

Robert Ray

ADC was created by County Commissioners' resolution on 11/18/1980. Meetings of an agricultural task force started in 1976 and can be seen as the early years of an informal ADC.

Table of Contents

Introduction

The Bounty of Chester County: Heritage Edition was written to celebrate the rich heritage we have in the agriculture that surrounds us. The three hundred years of history we see in Chester County are reminders of those farmers and others who have preserved the soil as well as a way of life. Strong stone walls surrounding rolling fields and the remains of gristmills that dot the countryside all contribute to this feeling of stability and deep roots.

Chester County is a blending of many ethnic groups: Swiss, Swiss-German, Scots, Welsh, plus English and Irish Quakers. As immigrants entered the "new world" some proceeded to move across the country in search of their fortune. But many stayed and have given us a wealth of culture and special recipes they prepared for their families. During the nineteenth century, farm laborers and mill workers from Europe and Africa added their native culture foodways. The Italians brought their pasta recipes and greatly contributed to the mushroom industry as we know it.

There were gristmills located along the many creeks of the county, and they had a lot to do with how we eat today. It was there that new techniques of milling brought new uses for the grains that were grown. As farmers moved from rye to wheat, and found the special wheat that produces those infamous pretzels, they were always open to new ideas. The gristmill was a "community center" of that time, with lots of exchange between neighbors. Pennsylvania Dutch women roasted their own corn in the cookstove and took it to the mill to have it ground into cornmeal.

The recipes included in this book came from all facets of Chester County, including the farm community. Century Farm owners, celebrating more than one hundred years of agriculture in their family, shared their favorites. Some recipes are from the preserved cookbooks of past generations.

Chester County is a growing county and we have acquired different tastes as well as the need to save time in preparing foods. These have been addressed in this book with newer recipes and preparation techniques. The slow cooker, microwave, food processor, and a grill have found their way into kitchens today and we have recipes that use them. The Fruit and Wine chapter includes popular Chester County wines to be used in fruit punches.

You will find the recipes divided according to the commodity they represent. The various chapters promote our abundance of fresh, available food in Chester County. The Brandywine Valley is considered the Mushroom Capital of the World, and we are proud to have a chapter for the white mushrooms as well as the exotics. You will find many new and exciting ways to use the staples of milk, eggs, beef, pork, lamb, and poultry in your menus. There are even recipes for duck and seafood.

Jane Davidson, Chester County Heritage Preservation Coordinator, has contributed greatly to this book by documenting the gristmills that operated in Chester County during the past centuries. Special thanks to the Chester County Historical Society for the use of their historical pictures.

This chapter is completed with recipes for breads, pastas, and cakes that use different kinds of flour.

This cookbook would not have been possible without the invaluable cooperation of the cooks of Chester County. We realize that what makes a recipe special is not only the taste but the recollection of Aunt Mary or Grandma as they prepared their pumpkin pie or biscuits.

A special thank you to the Family and Consumer Sciences Association for testing the recipes and adding many of their own tried-and-true ones. Our husbands deserve our thanks for their patience and the encouragement they gave us during this project.

We appreciate the support of the Chester County Commissioners and the Pennsylvania State Representatives and Senators. Their favorite recipes are included in this collection.

As we look to the future of Chester County agriculture, may we always remember those who produced the food that makes our county great. As we preserve the land, we must continue to support the farmers. The land without an efficient farmer will grow up into a jungle. May Chester County continue to be one of the top agriculture counties in the United States.

Betty A. Collins
Joyce E. Hershey
Editors

IN 1940, PUMPING WATER WAS A DAILY CHORE AT THE LYNDELL POST OFFICE AND PIONEER CASH GROCERY STORE, EAST BRANDYWINE TOWNSHIP.

County Of Chester

Citation

WHEREAS,
More than 176,000 acres or 36% of Chester County's total acreage is in active farming and its countryside is dotted by approximately 1,880 farms with an average size of 126 acres; and

WHEREAS,
Because of fertile soil, favorable climate conditions and advanced farming practices, a diverse agrarian economy is present consisting of dairies, mushrooms, beef, poultry, grains, produce, aqua culture, pork, nurseries and fruit; and

WHEREAS,
Chester County is number one in the Commonwealth of Pennsylvania in crop yield and cash receipts of agricultural crops; and

WHEREAS,
Substantial agri-business supports the farming economy through processing and/or distribution.

NOW, THEREFORE, BE IT RESOLVED, By the Board of Commissioners, County of Chester, Commonwealth of Pennsylvania, that we hereby recognize _The Bounty of Chester County, Heritage Edition,_ as the official cookbook to enhance the value that Chester County's agriculture products contribute to Chester County's economy.

IN SO DOING,
We applaud Chester County's Agricultural Development Council and all Chester County farmers for teaming together in a public-private partnership endeavor that will enhance heritage awareness and promote the benefits of fresh farm products to all Chester County citizens.

_____
Karen L. Martynick, Chairman

_____
Colin A. Hanna, Commissioner

_____
Andrew E. Dinniman, Commissioner

White Mushrooms

SPONSOR: COMMUNITY AWARENESS COMMITTEE (AMERICAN MUSHROOM INSTITUTE)

White mushrooms are ready to be picked inside a darkened mushroom house.

The American Mushroom Institute (AMI) is a national voluntary trade association representing the growers, processors, suppliers, and marketers of mushrooms in the United States. Community Awareness Committee (CAC), a committee of AMI, represents and addresses the challenges of the local Chester County mushroom industry through educational, environmental, and impact awareness. CAC's goal is to maintain the local mushroom industry as an asset to the community.

Mushrooms have always possessed a magical quality. Their unique shapes and colors fascinate us. Most importantly, the mushroom boasts a delicious taste, versatility, and nutritional value. It's a magic that turns the simplest recipe into an extraordinary dish.

The cultivation of mushrooms in America began in 1896 when William Swayne of Kennett Square became the first person to build a house used exclusively for growing mushrooms. Since that humble beginning, Chester County has become the Mushroom Capital of the United States. More than 25 percent of the mushrooms cultivated in the United States are grown in southern Chester County, Pennsylvania. Mushroom sales in Pennsylvania represent the state's largest cash crop. If you want to know more about our industry, contact the AMI-CAC office in Avondale, Pennsylvania, at 610-268-7483.

LEFT TO RIGHT: FRESH PICKED MUSHROOMS READY FOR MARKET.
MUSHROOM HOUSES IN NEW GARDEN TOWNSHIP.
MUSHROOMS ARE GROWN IN TIERS OF BEDS.

Mushroom Yogurt Dip

2 tablespoons butter
1/2 cup finely chopped fresh
   mushrooms
2 green onions, finely chopped
3 ounces cream cheese,
   softened

1/2 cup plain yogurt
1 tablespoon chopped
   fresh dill
1 teaspoon crushed garlic

Combine the butter, mushrooms and green onions in a small microwave-safe bowl. Microwave on High for 3 minutes. Add the cream cheese. Microwave for 3 minutes. Add the yogurt, dill and garlic and mix well. Chill, covered, for 2 hours or longer. Serve with assorted vegetables for dipping.

Yield: 2 cups dip

Mushroom Spread

4 slices bacon
8 ounces fresh mushrooms,
   chopped
1 small onion, finely chopped
1 garlic clove, minced
2 tablespoons flour
1/4 teaspoon salt

1/8 teaspoon pepper
8 ounces cream cheese,
   softened
2 teaspoons
   Worcestershire sauce
1 teaspoon soy sauce
1/2 cup sour cream

Cook the bacon in a skillet until crisp. Remove the bacon to paper towels to drain. Crumble the bacon. Drain the skillet, reserving 2 tablespoons bacon drippings. Sauté the mushrooms, onion and garlic in the reserved drippings until tender. Stir in the flour, salt and pepper. Add the cream cheese, Worcestershire sauce and soy sauce. Cook until the cream cheese is melted, stirring constantly. Stir in the sour cream and bacon. Cook until heated through. Serve warm with small bread rounds or crackers.

Yield: 2 1/2 cups spread

DILL AND YOGURT DIP

Combine 1/2 cup plain lowfat yogurt, 2 tablespoons mayonnaise, 1 tablespoon finely chopped scallions, 1 tablespoon chopped fresh dill, 1 teaspoon lemon juice, 1/4 teaspoon salt and 1/8 teaspoon pepper in a small bowl and mix well. Serve with halved or sliced mushrooms for dipping.

Yield: 3/4 cup dip

SPICY DIPPING
SAUCE

Combine 1 cup
mayonnaise-type
salad dressing or
mayonnaise,
2 tablespoons
steak sauce and
2 teaspoons garlic
powder in a bowl
and mix well. Serve
with halved or
whole mushrooms
for dipping.

Yield: 1 cup sauce

Mushroom Pâté

8 ounces fresh mushrooms,
  chopped
2 tablespoons butter or
  margarine
8 ounces cream cheese,
  softened

1 tablespoon dry white
  wine
1 teaspoon lemon juice
1/4 teaspoon garlic powder
Hot pepper sauce to taste

Sauté the mushrooms in the butter in a skillet until the liquid
evaporates. Process the cream cheese, wine, lemon juice, garlic
powder and hot pepper sauce in a blender until smooth. Add the
sautéed mushrooms and blend well. Chill, covered, until ready to
serve. Serve with crackers.

Yield: 2 cups spread

Marinated Mushrooms

1/4 cup white vinegar
1/4 cup water
1/2 teaspoon salt
1/4 teaspoon pepper
1 bay leaf
1 pound small button
  mushrooms
3/4 cup red wine vinegar
1/4 cup water

1/2 cup vegetable oil
1 bay leaf
1 garlic clove
1/2 teaspoon sugar
1/2 teaspoon parsley
1/8 teaspoon oregano
Salt and pepper to taste
Chopped onion to taste

Combine the white vinegar, 1/4 cup water, 1/2 teaspoon salt,
1/4 teaspoon pepper and 1 bay leaf in a saucepan and mix well.
Add the mushrooms. Bring to a boil. Boil for 10 minutes. Drain,
discarding the bay leaf. Combine the red wine vinegar, 1/4 cup
water, oil, 1 bay leaf, garlic, sugar, parsley, oregano and salt and
pepper to taste in a bowl and mix well. Stir in the onion. Add the
mushrooms and toss to coat. Marinate, covered, in the refrigerator.
Remove the bay leaf before serving. Serve with wooden picks.

Yield: 8 servings

Stuffed Mushroom Caps

12 large whole mushrooms
2 tablespoons vegetable oil
1 small onion, finely chopped
4 ounces ground chuck
2 slices prosciutto, coarsely chopped
1/3 cup dry sherry
1/4 cup dry bread crumbs
1 teaspoon garlic powder
1 teaspoon salt
1/2 teaspoon pepper
1/4 cup grated Parmesan cheese

Remove the stems from the mushrooms. Chop the stems finely. Place the mushroom caps on a baking sheet. Heat the oil in a large skillet over medium heat. Add the onion and ground chuck. Cook until the ground chuck is brown and crumbly. Add the chopped stems, prosciutto and sherry. Cook for 5 minutes. Add the bread crumbs, garlic powder, salt and pepper and mix well. Stuff into the mushroom caps. Sprinkle with the Parmesan cheese. Broil 3 inches from the heat source for 5 minutes. Serve immediately.

Yield: 12 servings

Sausage-Stuffed Mushrooms

24 gourmet mushrooms
8 ounces Italian sausage, casing removed
1/4 cup finely chopped onion
1 medium garlic clove, minced
1/4 cup shredded provolone cheese
1/4 cup dry fine Italian bread crumbs
1 egg, lightly beaten
2 tablespoons butter or margarine, melted

Remove the stems from the mushroom caps. Chop the stems. Brown the sausage, chopped mushroom stems, onion and garlic in a 10-inch skillet over medium heat, stirring until the sausage is crumbly; drain. Stir in the cheese, bread crumbs and egg.

Brush the mushroom caps with the butter. Place on a rack in a broiler pan. Spoon about 2 teaspoons of the sausage mixture into each mushroom cap. Broil 4 inches from the heat source for 5 minutes or until heated through.

Yield: 24 servings

WORKERS CLEAN MUSHROOMS AND
PREPARE THEM FOR CANNING AT E. H.
JACOB COMPANY, WEST GOSHEN
TOWNSHIP, 1933.

Mushroom Cheese Nuggets

"THIS RECIPE ORIGINALLY CALLED FOR OLIVES, BUT SINCE I'M NOT SURE OLIVES ARE REALLY GROWN IN CHESTER COUNTY, I'VE ADAPTED THE RECIPE TO SUIT OUR WONDERFUL CHESTER COUNTY MUSHROOMS! IT IS ALSO ESPECIALLY ADVISABLE TO USE OUR EXCELLENT CHESTER COUNTY CHEDDAR CHEESE AND BUTTER!" —COMMISSIONER ANDY DINNIMAN

4 ounces Cheddar cheese, shredded, softened
1/4 cup (1/2 stick) butter, softened
3/4 cup sifted flour
1/8 teaspoon salt
1/2 teaspoon paprika
36 to 40 small to medium mushrooms
1/4 cup (1/2 stick) butter
Garlic salt to taste

Mix the cheese and 1/4 cup butter in a bowl. Add the flour, salt and paprika. Mix to form a soft dough. Sauté the mushrooms in 1/4 cup butter in a skillet until tender. Sprinkle with garlic salt. Let stand until cool. Flatten a small amount of the dough at a time and wrap around each mushroom. Place on ungreased baking sheets.

Bake at 400 degrees for 12 to 15 minutes or until light brown. Serve hot or cold with cocktail sauce or spicy salsa. You may prepare in advance, chill or freeze, and bake later.

Yield: 36 to 40 servings

Cheesy Mushroom Canapés

MUSHROOM CARE AND HANDLING

* Do not peel mushrooms or you will lose out on lots of good flavor and vitamin content.
* Rinse mushrooms lightly because they absorb water.
* Do not overcook mushrooms. A good rule to follow is to cook mushrooms for about 10 minutes to avoid drying.
* Store mushrooms in a nonrecycled paper bag in the refrigerator. Storing in a plastic bag accelerates deterioration.

1 pound mushrooms, finely chopped
2 tablespoons butter or margarine
2 tablespoons flour
$1/4$ teaspoon salt
$1/8$ teaspoon pepper
$1/2$ cup milk
1 cup shredded Swiss or Gruyère cheese
24 party rye bread slices, toasted, or crackers

Sauté the mushrooms in the butter in a 10-inch skillet over medium heat until tender and the liquid is evaporated. Stir in the flour, salt and pepper. Cook for 1 minute, stirring constantly. Stir in the milk gradually. Bring to a boil. Cook until thickened, stirring frequently. Stir in $1/2$ cup of the cheese.

Spread 1 tablespoon mushroom mixture on each bread slice. Arrange on a rack in a broiler pan. Sprinkle with the remaining cheese. Broil 4 inches from the heat source for 3 minutes or until hot and bubbly. Garnish with chopped fresh parsley.

Yield: 24 servings

Chester County Mushroom Tapenade

1 cup black olives, finely chopped
3 garlic cloves, minced
3 ounces sun-dried tomatoes, chopped
3 to 4 tablespoons pesto
6 ounces button mushrooms, finely chopped
6 ounces cremini mushrooms, finely chopped
1 cup virgin olive oil
1/2 cup freshly grated Romano cheese
1 (17-ounce) package frozen puff pastry, thawed
1 egg, beaten

Combine the olives, garlic, sun-dried tomatoes and pesto in a large bowl and mix well. Sauté the mushrooms in the olive oil in a skillet for 2 to 3 minutes or until soft. Drain the mushrooms, reserving the liquid. Add the olive mixture to the mushrooms and mix well. Cook over medium heat for 5 minutes. Remove from the heat. Stir in the cheese. Add enough of the reserved mushroom liquid to keep the mixture moist.

Prepare the puff pastry using the package directions. Cut into twenty-four 4-inch squares. Keep covered with a damp cloth. Place 1 to 2 tablespoons of the filling in the center of each square. Mold each into a pyramid shape, pinching all sides to secure and enclose the filling. Brush with the egg. Place on a baking sheet. Bake at 300 degrees for 15 to 20 minutes or until golden brown.

Yield: 24 servings

Mushroom Barley Soup

³/₄ cup chopped onion
¹/₂ cup chopped carrots
¹/₂ cup chopped celery
1 teaspoon minced garlic
1¹/₂ tablespoons butter
8 ounces sliced mushrooms
¹/₂ teaspoon thyme
Salt and pepper to taste
6 cups chicken broth
¹/₂ cup barley

Sauté the onion, carrots, celery and garlic in the butter in a skillet until tender but not brown. Add the mushrooms. Sauté until tender. Sprinkle with the thyme, salt and pepper. Add the broth and barley. Bring to a boil and reduce the heat. Simmer for 2 hours or until the barley is tender. Ladle into soup bowls. Garnish with dill and chopped parsley.

Yield: 6 servings

Creamed Mushrooms

10 ounces fresh mushrooms
2 tablespoons butter
2 tablespoons flour
2 tablespoons milk
1 (5-ounce) can evaporated milk
Salt and pepper to taste

Rinse the mushrooms gently in cold water. Cut the mushrooms into thin slices. Bring the mushrooms and butter to a boil in a saucepan and reduce the heat. Simmer, covered, for 3 minutes. Do not overcook. Mix the flour and milk in a bowl to form a paste. Stir into the mushrooms. Cook over low heat until thick and bubbly. Cook for 1 minute longer. Stir in the evaporated milk. Season with salt and pepper. Serve with turkey, ham or roast beef.

Yield: 6 servings

Mushrooms with Bay Leaf, Cinnamon and Garlic

1 1/4 pounds button mushrooms
4 cups water
Juice of 1 lemon
1 bay leaf
1 cinnamon stick
6 tablespoons olive oil
1/4 teaspoon salt
10 black peppercorns, bruised
3/4 cup finely chopped parsley
1 garlic clove, finely chopped

Rinse the mushrooms under cold running water and pat dry. Bring 4 cups water, 1/2 of the lemon juice, bay leaf and cinnamon stick to a boil in a saucepan. Add the mushrooms and enough additional water to cover. Boil for 2 to 3 minutes. Drain the mushrooms, discarding the bay leaf and cinnamon stick. Place the mushrooms, olive oil, remaining lemon juice, salt and peppercorns in a skillet. Cook for 15 minutes. Remove from the heat. Drain and cool. Sprinkle with the parsley and garlic just before serving.

Yield: 8 servings

Sautéed Mushroom Teriyaki

8 ounces sliced white button mushrooms or sliced portobella mushrooms
2 tablespoons olive oil
1/4 cup teriyaki sauce
Garlic salt to taste

Sauté the mushrooms in the olive oil in a skillet until tender. Add the teriyaki sauce and garlic salt. Sauté until heated through.

Yield: 2 servings

Mushroom and Wild Rice Casserole

SAMUEL E. HAYES, JR., SECRETARY OF AGRICULTURE, COMMONWEALTH OF PENNSYLVANIA

2 (4-ounce) packages long-grain and wild rice mix
3 tablespoons butter
1 cup chopped celery
1/2 cup chopped onion
1 pound chopped fresh mushrooms
1 (10-ounce) can cream of mushroom soup
Salt and pepper to taste

Cook the rice mix using the package directions. Melt the butter in a skillet. Add the celery and onion. Sauté for 5 minutes. Add the mushrooms. Sauté for 6 to 8 minutes or until tender. Stir into the cooked rice. Add the soup, salt and pepper and mix well. Pour into a buttered casserole.

Bake at 350 degrees for 20 minutes or until bubbly. For a creamier dish, you may add an additional 1/2 can of mushroom soup.

Yield: 10 to 12 servings

MUSHROOM YIELDS

* 1 pound whole mushrooms, uncooked, yields about 6 cups sliced, or 5 cups chopped
* 1 pound sliced mushrooms, cooked, yields about 2 cups
* 1 pound chopped mushrooms, cooked, yields about 2 cups

Mushroom and Green Onion Egg Bake

4 ounces mushrooms, sliced	6 eggs
4 green onions, chopped	2 tablespoons flour
1 tablespoon vegetable oil	$1/4$ teaspoon salt
1 cup reduced-fat cottage cheese	$1/8$ teaspoon freshly ground pepper
1 cup sour cream	$1/8$ teaspoon hot pepper sauce

Sauté the mushrooms and green onions in the hot oil in a medium skillet over medium heat until tender. Remove from the heat. Process the cottage cheese in a food processor or blender until almost smooth. Add the sour cream, eggs, flour, salt, pepper and hot pepper sauce and process until blended. Add to the sautéed mushroom mixture and mix well. Pour into a greased 1-quart shallow baking dish. Bake at 350 degrees for 40 minutes or until a knife inserted near the center comes out clean.

Yield: 6 servings

Swiss Mushrooms

1 pound sliced mushrooms	1 (5-ounce) can evaporated milk
3 medium onions, sliced	2 teaspoons soy sauce
2 tablespoons butter	6 to 8 ($1/2$-inch-thick) slices French
1 cup shredded Swiss cheese	bread
1 (10-ounce) can cream of	6 to 8 thin slices Swiss cheese
mushroom soup	

Sauté the mushrooms and onions in the butter in a skillet until tender. Place in a $7^{1}/_{2}{\times}12$-inch baking dish. Sprinkle with the shredded Swiss cheese. Mix the soup, evaporated milk and soy sauce in a bowl. Pour over the shredded cheese. Layer the bread and Swiss cheese slices over the top. Chill, covered, in the refrigerator for 4 to 12 hours. Bake, loosely covered, at 375 degrees for 30 minutes. Uncover and bake for 15 minutes longer. Let stand for 5 minutes before serving.

Yield: 6 servings

Boeuf en *Croûte* avec *Duxelles*
(Beef in Crust with Mushroom Mixture)

1 (4-pound) beef tenderloin
16 ounces fresh mushrooms, finely chopped
1/4 cup finely chopped onion
2 tablespoons butter or margarine
2 tablespoons brandy or port
1 tablespoon chopped fresh parsley
1/8 teaspoon salt

1/8 teaspoon pepper
1 (17-ounce) package frozen puff
    pastry, thawed
1 egg white, beaten
1 egg yolk, beaten
1 teaspoon milk
Chasseur Sauce

Place the beef on a rack in a roasting pan. Bake at 450 degrees for 30 minutes or until a meat thermometer registers 120 degrees when inserted in the center. Remove from the oven and cool to room temperature. Sauté the mushrooms and onion in the hot butter in a 10-inch skillet over medium heat until tender and the liquid is evaporated. Stir in the brandy, parsley, salt and pepper. Simmer for 1 minute. Cool to room temperature. Unfold the puff pastry sheets on a floured surface. Press the long edges together to form 1 large piece. Roll into a rectangle large enough to encase the beef. Trim the pastry, reserving the trimmings. Brush with some of the egg white. Spread the mushroom mixture on the pastry to within 2 inches of the edges. Place the beef in the center. Fold the pastry around the beef, sealing the edges with some remaining egg white. Place seam side down on a 10×15-inch baking pan. Cut the reserved trimmings into shapes and arrange on top. Brush with the remaining egg white. Brush with a mixture of the egg yolk and milk. Bake at 425 degrees for 20 minutes or until golden brown. Let stand for 10 minutes. Serve with Chasseur Sauce.

Yield: 8 servings

Chasseur Sauce

3 ounces shiitake mushrooms, chopped
3 tablespoons chopped shallots
1/4 teaspoon crushed tarragon leaves
3 tablespoons butter or margarine

1/4 cup chablis or other dry white wine
1 (10-ounce) can beef gravy
1/2 cup tomato sauce
2 tablespoons chopped fresh parsley

Sauté the mushrooms, shallots and tarragon in the butter in a 10-inch skillet over medium heat until tender. Add the wine. Cook until most of the liquid is evaporated. Add the gravy and tomato sauce. Cook until heated through, stirring occasionally. Stir in the parsley.

Yield: 1 3/4 cups sauce

Beef Stroganoff

1¹/₂ cups finely chopped onions
¹/₃ cup butter
1¹/₂ pounds fresh mushrooms, sliced
¹/₃ cup butter
3¹/₂ pounds beef top round, cut into ¹/₄×2-inch strips
6 tablespoons flour
¹/₃ cup butter
3 cups bouillon
1¹/₂ teaspoons salt
6 tablespoons tomato paste
2 teaspoons Worcestershire sauce
³/₄ cup sour cream
1¹/₂ cups heavy cream
8 cups hot cooked rice

Sauté the onions in ¹/₃ cup butter in a large saucepan until golden brown. Remove the onions to a bowl. Sauté the mushrooms in ¹/₃ cup butter in the saucepan until light brown. Remove the mushrooms to a bowl. Coat the beef with the flour. Sauté the beef in ¹/₃ cup butter in the saucepan until brown. Add the bouillon, salt and sautéed onions.

Simmer, covered, for 1¹/₂ hours or until the beef is tender. Add the tomato paste, Worcestershire sauce, sour cream, heavy cream and the sautéed mushrooms. Cook until heated through. Serve over the rice.

Yield: 10 to 12 servings

SELECTING THE PERFECT MUSHROOM

Look for smooth, firm closed mushrooms when purchasing fresh mushrooms. Mushrooms are available in three sizes: small, medium, and large. Small and medium mushrooms are generally used in salads and sautés. The large mushrooms are served stuffed or broiled, or in soups and stews. Agaricus bisporus, the traditional market variety, is the largest crop of mushrooms produced. Mushrooms grown in the United States are either white or brown in color; however, there is little difference in the taste or texture.

Herbed Lemon Chicken with Mushrooms

12 ounces white mushrooms, sliced
1/2 teaspoon minced garlic
2 tablespoons chicken broth or water
4 boneless skinless chicken breasts, flattened
3 tablespoons fresh lemon juice
1/8 teaspoon crushed tarragon leaves
1/8 teaspoon pepper
1 pound fresh tomatoes, chopped

Combine the mushrooms, garlic and broth in a large skillet. Bring to a boil and reduce the heat. Simmer, covered, for 2 minutes. Uncover and simmer for 3 minutes longer. Add the chicken, lemon juice, tarragon and pepper. Simmer, uncovered, for 10 minutes or until the chicken is nearly cooked through, basting occasionally with the broth. Add the tomatoes. Cook for 5 minutes or until the chicken is cooked through and the tomatoes are slightly softened.

Yield: 4 servings

THE INTERIOR OF E. H. JACOB
COMPANY'S MUSHROOM HOUSE IN 1933
SHOWS TIERS OF MUSHROOM BEDS
AND BASKETS OF PICKED MUSHROOMS,
WEST GOSHEN TOWNSHIP.

Ginger Mushroom Stir-Fry

3 tablespoons lemon juice
3 tablespoons soy sauce
1 tablespoon grated fresh gingerroot
2 garlic cloves, pressed
2 boneless skinless chicken breasts, cut into strips ¹/₂ inch thick
2 teaspoons cornstarch
¹/₃ cup chicken broth or bouillon
1 to 2 tablespoons vegetable oil
8 ounces fresh mushrooms, quartered
1¹/₂ cups asparagus or green bean slices, about 1¹/₂ inches long
3 green onions, sliced diagonally into 1-inch pieces
Toasted sesame seeds

Mix the lemon juice, soy sauce, gingerroot and garlic in a bowl. Add the chicken and toss to coat. Dissolve the cornstarch in the broth in a bowl. Heat the oil in a wok or skillet until sizzling. Drain the chicken, reserving the marinade. Add the chicken and mushrooms to the wok. Stir-fry over high heat until the chicken is no longer pink. Add the asparagus and green onions. Stir-fry until the chicken juices run clear and the vegetables are tender-crisp. Stir in the broth mixture and reserved marinade. Simmer for 3 minutes. Sprinkle with sesame seeds. Serve over hot cooked rice. Garnish with lemon slices and cilantro.

Yield: 4 servings

Susanna Foo's Mushroom Pancakes

SUSANNA FOO, CHEF-OWNER, PHILADELPHIA, PENNSYLVANIA

1/4 cup vegetable oil
4 slices bacon, finely chopped
2 pounds fresh white mushrooms, finely chopped
1/2 cup finely chopped peeled fresh shrimp
1 tablespoon kosher salt
1/2 teaspoon pepper
4 bunches scallions, finely chopped
1/2 cup finely chopped fresh coriander
20 (6-inch) flour tortillas
4 egg yolks, lightly beaten
2 tablespoons vegetable oil

Heat 1/4 cup oil in a medium skillet. Add the bacon. Cook until golden brown. Add the mushrooms. Cook for 5 minutes. Add the shrimp, kosher salt and pepper. Cook until the shrimp turn pink. Remove from the heat and strain the liquid. Add the scallions and coriander and mix well.

Brush the rim of a tortilla with the egg yolks. Spoon 3 tablespoons of the mushroom mixture in the center. Top with a tortilla and seal the edges. Repeat the process, reserving each filled pancake on waxed paper until ready to cook.

Heat 2 tablespoons oil in a 10-inch skillet over medium heat. Cook each pancake for 3 minutes per side or until golden brown and crisp. Cut each pancake into quarters and serve immediately.

Yield: 10 servings

Exotic Mushrooms

SPONSOR: PHILLIPS MUSHROOM FARMS

Exotic mushrooms: clockwise from upper left, Maitake, Beech, Oyster, Shiitake, Pom Pom, Royal Trumpet.

Commercial mushroom cultivation started in Kennett Square, Pennsylvania, in 1896. From the beginning, Pennsylvania has played a major role in mushroom production and currently supplies 50 percent of the nearly 868 million pounds produced in the United States in 1999. Approximately 74 percent of the mushrooms produced are sold fresh; the remainder are processed for various products.

Phillips Mushroom Farms is a third-generation, family-owned business. It was started in 1926 by the family patriarch, William W. Phillips. In 1962, sons Donald P. and R. Marshall made Phillips one of the first mushroom companies to go direct from farm to market, packaging white mushrooms in small cartons for the consumer.

In 1979, Phillips was the first commercial farm to grow shiitake mushrooms for the fresh market. Production and marketing of other varieties of specialty mushrooms continued over the years. In 1985, Phillips Mushroom Farms introduced the "portobella" to consumers. Growing, packaging, and shipping more than 30 million pounds of nine varieties of mushrooms earns them the title of largest specialty mushroom producer in the United States. They employ 240 people full time and are located in Kennett Square, Pennsylvania.

Phillips Mushroom Place, a gift shop and mushroom museum, is located on U.S. Route 1, one-half mile south of Longwood Gardens. The Mushroom Place offers mushroom gifts and specialty items for the fungiphile, with a museum featuring a diorama and short video detailing the history of the industry. A mushroom-growing display is also part of the museum.

CLOCKWISE FROM UPPER LEFT: ROYAL TRUMPET MUSHROOMS, SHIITAKE MUSHROOMS, BEECH MUSHROOMS, OYSTER MUSHROOMS, POM POM MUSHROOMS, PORTOBELLA MUSHROOMS (CENTER), ENOKI MUSHROOMS, CRIMINI MUSHROOMS AND MAITAKE MUSHROOMS. RURAL LANDSCAPE IN WEST MARLBOROUGH TOWNSHIP.

Grilled Portobella Mushroom with Goat Cheese

TERRACE RESTAURANT AT LONGWOOD GARDENS

1 portobella mushroom
1 tablespoon olive oil
Salt and pepper to taste
1 garlic clove, roasted
3 fresh basil leaves

2 sprigs of thyme
2 sprigs of parsley
2 ounces Montrachet cheese
   (goat cheese)

Trim the stem from the underside of the mushroom. Brush with the olive oil. Season with salt and pepper. Process the garlic, basil, thyme and parsley in a food processor until finely chopped. Add the cheese and process until blended. Do not over process. Spoon into the mushroom cap. Place on a baking sheet. Broil until the cheese mixture is light brown.

Yield: 1 serving

Kennett Square Mushroom Strudel

TERRACE RESTAURANT AT LONGWOOD GARDENS

2 pounds shiitake mushrooms, chopped
2 pounds trumpet mushrooms, chopped
2 pounds oyster mushrooms, chopped
1 pound medium button mushrooms,
   chopped
2 teaspoons chopped shallots
2 tablespoons butter

3 ounces dried tarragon, or
   5 ounces fresh tarragon, chopped
Salt and pepper to taste
1/2 cup madeira
4 ounces bread crumbs
6 sheets phyllo dough
1/4 cup (1/2 stick) butter, melted

Sauté the mushrooms and shallots in 2 tablespoons butter in a skillet for 5 to 8 minutes or until tender. Sprinkle with the tarragon, salt and pepper. Add the wine. Cook until the liquid is evaporated, stirring to deglaze the skillet. Remove from the heat. Chill in the refrigerator. Combine the mushroom mixture with enough of the bread crumbs to shape into a ball. Stack 2 sheets of the phyllo together and brush with melted butter. Repeat the process twice, layering to form a stack of 6 layers. Spread with the mushroom mixture and roll up. Place on a baking sheet. Brush with the remaining melted butter. Bake at 350 degrees for 15 to 25 minutes or until golden brown.

Yield: 8 servings

Mushroom Onion Soup

4 large portobella mushroom caps
3 large Spanish onions, thinly sliced
3 tablespoons butter
Leaves of 1 stalk celery, finely chopped
$^1/_2$ cup sherry
Basil, parsley and seasoned salt to taste
1 (14-ounce) can reduced-sodium fat-free chicken broth
1 (14-ounce) can beef broth
Parmesan cheese to taste

Cut each mushroom into strips. Cut each strip into 4 pieces. Sauté the onions in melted butter in a skillet until transparent. Add the mushrooms and celery leaves. Sauté over medium-low heat. Add the sherry. Sprinkle with basil, parsley and seasoned salt. Cook until the vegetables are tender. Add the chicken broth and beef broth. Cook until heated through. Ladle into soup bowls. Sprinkle with Parmesan cheese. Serve with croutons.

Yield: 4 servings

Buckley's Tavern Wild Mushroom Soup

BUCKLEY'S TAVERN, WILMINGTON, DELAWARE

1 bunch leeks
1/2 cup olive oil
2 pounds assorted wild and specialty mushrooms (such as oyster,
    shiitake, portobella, chanterelles or lobster), rinsed, sliced
1 1/2 pounds cremini mushrooms, sliced
5 quarts chicken stock
4 cups canned diced tomatoes
1 cup sherry
1 tablespoon minced garlic
1/2 cup chopped fresh parsley
1/2 cup chopped fresh basil leaves
Salt and pepper to taste

Trim the leeks, leaving a few inches of the green stems. Rinse and cut into thin slices. Sauté the leeks in the olive oil in a skillet until soft. Add the mushrooms. Sauté just until the mushrooms begin to lose their liquid. Add the chicken stock, tomatoes, sherry and garlic. Bring to a boil and reduce the heat. Simmer for 30 minutes. Add the parsley, basil, salt and pepper. Simmer for 5 minutes. Ladle into soup bowls and serve with a crusty peasant bread.

Yield: 16 to 18 servings

CREMINI, OR ITALIAN BROWN, MUSHROOM

The cremini mushroom, a cousin to the popular white mushroom, is light tan to dark brown in color and provides a deeper earthier flavor than the white mushroom. Cremini mushrooms are wonderful cooked, stuffed, sautéed or used as an ingredient. You may substitute cremini mushrooms for the traditional button mushrooms, but reduce the quantity slightly to compensate for their richer flavor. Store all exotic mushrooms in the refrigerator in their pre-pack trays or in a bowl covered with a slightly damp towel. Rinse gently before using.

Chester County Mushroom Soup

TERRACE RESTAURANT AT LONGWOOD GARDENS

1 medium carrot
1/2 medium onion
2 ribs celery
1 tablespoon butter or vegetable oil
2 pounds button mushrooms, rinsed
8 ounces shiitake mushrooms, rinsed
8 ounces oyster mushrooms, rinsed
1 tablespoon chopped fresh tarragon

1 teaspoon salt
1 teaspoon white pepper
6 cups chicken or vegetable stock
2 cups heavy cream
2 tablespoons melted butter or
    vegetable oil
2 tablespoons flour
Salt and white pepper to taste

Process the carrot, onion and celery in a food processor until minced. Sauté the vegetables in 1 tablespoon butter in a heavy stockpot. Process the mushrooms in a food processor until minced. Add to the sautéed vegetables. Sprinkle with tarragon, 1 teaspoon salt and 1 teaspoon white pepper. Cook for 15 minutes. Do not burn. Add the chicken stock and cream. Bring to a boil. Mix 2 tablespoons melted butter and flour in a bowl until smooth. Add to the soup and mix well. Return to a boil. Cook until thickened, stirring constantly. Reduce the heat. Simmer for 30 minutes. Season with salt and white pepper to taste.

Yield: 16 servings

Cream of Cremini and Shrimp Soup

HUGO'S INN, KENNETT SQUARE, PENNSYLVANIA

8 ounces peeled shrimp, chopped
1 tablespoon butter
2 (10-ounce) cans tomato soup

1/4 to 1/2 cup medium cream or milk
8 ounces sliced cremini mushrooms
Chopped fresh parsley

Sauté the shrimp in the butter in a skillet until barely cooked. Bring the soup and cream to a simmer in a saucepan. Add the mushrooms and shrimp with pan juices. Simmer for 5 to 10 minutes or until the shrimp are cooked through. Ladle into soup bowls. Sprinkle with parsley.

Yield: 3 servings

Portobella Mushroom Salad

1 head butter lettuce
6 Grilled Portobellas, sliced
6 ounces goat cheese, crumbled

1 cup toasted skinned hazelnuts
$^1/_2$ cup Balsamic Vinaigrette

Tear the lettuce into bite-size pieces and place in a salad bowl. Layer the mushroom slices over the lettuce. Sprinkle with the goat cheese and hazelnuts. Drizzle with the Balsamic Vinaigrette. You may add 3 tablespoons mayonnaise to the Balsamic Vinaigrette for a creamier version.

Yield: 6 servings

Grilled Portobellas

6 whole portobella mushrooms, stems removed

$^1/_2$ cup Balsamic Vinaigrette

Arrange the mushrooms in a shallow baking dish. Pour the Balsamic Vinaigrette over the mushrooms. Marinate, covered, in the refrigerator for up to 24 hours, turning the mushrooms once. Drain the mushrooms, discarding the marinade. Place on a grill rack. Grill over warm coals for 5 to 10 minutes or until cooked through, turning once. To broil, place the mushrooms on a baking sheet and broil for 5 to 8 minutes. To bake, place the mushrooms in a baking dish and bake for 15 minutes.

Yield: 6 servings

Balsamic Vinaigrette

$^3/_4$ cup olive oil
$^1/_4$ cup vinegar
1 tablespoon balsamic vinegar
2 teaspoons lemon juice

1 teaspoon sugar
1 teaspoon salt
$^1/_4$ teaspoon pepper

Combine the olive oil, vinegar, balsamic vinegar, lemon juice, sugar, salt and pepper in a jar with a tight-fitting lid. Shake, covered, until blended.

Yield: 1 cup vinaigrette

Portobella Mushroom Sauté

6 ounces portobella mushrooms
2 garlic cloves, minced
2 tablespoons olive oil
2 tablespoons marsala
1/8 teaspoon oregano

1/8 teaspoon salt
1/8 teaspoon pepper
1 tablespoon bleu cheese
1 tablespoon butter

Sauté the mushrooms and garlic in the olive oil in a skillet over high heat. Add the wine, oregano, salt and pepper. Sauté until the mushrooms are tender. Add the bleu cheese and butter. Sauté until the sauce thickens.

Yield: 2 servings

Grilled Portobellas with Black Bean Salsa

THIS RECIPE IS A CREATION OF CHEF MICHAEL CARR FROM THE CHANCERY IN WEST CHESTER. HE GETS QUITE EXCITED WHEN TALKING ABOUT THIS DISH AND SWEARS IT'S TOO WONDERFUL FOR WORDS.

1 cup red wine
1/4 cup olive oil
1 small onion, chopped
1 tablespoon chopped garlic
1/2 teaspoon sage
1/2 teaspoon thyme
4 portobella mushroom caps
1 cup rinsed cooked black beans
1 cup chopped tomatoes

1 cup chopped yellow bell pepper
1 small red onion, chopped
1 bunch scallions, chopped
2 tablespoons finely chopped fresh
   cilantro
2 tablespoons lemon juice
2 tablespoons balsamic vinegar
1/2 tablespoon Tabasco sauce

Mix the wine, olive oil, onion, garlic, sage and thyme in a sealable plastic food storage bag. Add the mushrooms and seal the bag. Marinate in the refrigerator for 8 to 12 hours. Drain the mushrooms, discarding the marinade. Place the mushrooms on a grill rack. Grill until the mushrooms are tender.

Combine the black beans, tomatoes, bell pepper, red onion, scallions, cilantro, lemon juice, balsamic vinegar and Tabasco sauce in a bowl and mix well. Spoon into the mushrooms.

Yield: 4 servings

Polenta with Sautéed Mushrooms

1 cup milk
1 cup heavy cream
Salt to taste
4 ounces polenta
4 ounces shiitake mushrooms
2 tablespoons extra-virgin olive oil

½ shallot, chopped
1 tablespoon butter
2 tablespoons freshly grated
 Parmigiano-Reggiano
Chopped fresh chives to taste

Scald the milk and cream in a medium saucepan. Season with salt and remove from the heat. Add the polenta gradually, stirring constantly. Reduce the heat. Return the pan to the heat. Cook, covered, for 1 hour, stirring frequently. Remove the stems from the mushrooms, reserving the mushroom caps. Place the stems in a heatproof bowl and add enough boiling water to cover. Let stand for 20 minutes. Drain, reserving 1 cup mushroom stock and discarding the mushroom stems. Chop the reserved mushroom caps.

Heat the olive oil in a sauté pan until almost smoking. Add the shallot. Sauté until the shallot begins to caramelize. Add the chopped mushrooms. Sauté until the mushrooms begin to lose their juices. Add the reserved mushroom stock. Cook over medium-high heat until the liquid is reduced by ⅔.

Stir the butter and cheese into the polenta. Spoon onto serving plates. Spoon the sautéed mushrooms over the polenta and pour the pan juices over the top. Sprinkle with chives.

Yield: 4 to 6 servings

PHILLIPS MUSHROOM STORE,
MUSEUM AND GIFT SHOP ON
BALTIMORE PIKE, ROUTE ONE.

More Room for Mushroom No-Fat Chili

1 medium onion, chopped
3 garlic cloves, chopped
10 ounces white mushrooms, chopped
1/4 cup olive oil
8 ounces tofu
1/4 cup beef bouillon
2 large portobella mushrooms, coarsely chopped
32 ounces undrained canned red kidney beans
4 pounds canned tomatoes
1 (6-ounce) can tomato paste
2 tablespoons chili powder
1 teaspoon oregano
2 bay leaves
1/4 teaspoon cumin
1 teaspoon salt

Brown the onion, garlic and white mushrooms in the olive oil in a heavy stockpot over medium heat for 10 minutes. Combine the tofu and beef bouillon in a bowl and stir with a fork to blend well. Stir into the onion mixture. Add the portobella mushrooms. Cook for 10 minutes. Add the kidney beans, tomatoes and tomato paste and mix well. Stir in the chili powder, oregano, bay leaves, cumin and salt. Simmer over medium heat for 1 hour. Discard the bay leaves. Ladle into soup bowls. Garnish with enoki mushrooms and finely sliced red and green bell peppers.

Yield: 8 servings

Mushrooms Florentine

4 (3- to 4-inch) portobella
   mushrooms
Olive oil
Old Bay seasoning to taste
1 (9-ounce) package frozen
   creamed spinach, thawed

4 ounces grated sharp
   Cheddar cheese
12 pimento strips or
   roasted red bell
   pepper strips

Remove the stems from the mushrooms. Brush the mushrooms lightly with olive oil. Sprinkle with Old Bay seasoning. Place cap side up on a rack in a broiler pan. Broil 6 to 8 inches from the heat source for 8 to 10 minutes or until brown. Turn the mushrooms. Fill each mushroom cap with the creamed spinach. Sprinkle with the cheese. Top each with 3 pimento strips. Broil until the cheese melts.

Yield: 4 servings

Oyster Mushroom Omelet

3¹/₂ ounces oyster
   mushrooms, sliced
¹/₂ tablespoon margarine
4 eggs
2 tablespoons chopped scallions
   (green portion only)

¹/₈ teaspoon salt
¹/₈ teaspoon pepper
¹/₂ tablespoon margarine
1 cup shredded mozzarella
   cheese

Sauté the mushrooms in ¹/₂ tablespoon margarine in a skillet over medium-high heat for 3 minutes. Cover and remove from the heat. Beat the eggs, scallions, salt and pepper in a bowl. Melt ¹/₂ tablespoon margarine in a skillet over medium heat. Add the egg mixture. Cook until the egg mixture begins to set. Lift the edge, allowing the uncooked portion to flow underneath. Cook for 30 seconds. Sprinkle with the sautéed mushrooms and cheese. Fold in half. Cook for 1 minute. Place on a warm serving plate.

Yield: 2 servings

OYSTER MUSHROOMS

Oyster mushrooms are shaped like a shell or trumpet and are light beige, gray or soft brown in color. Their meaty texture and soft, smooth appearance make them a delightful addition to a variety of dishes; however, they are generally preferred cooked.

Portobella Tostada

1 1/2 pounds ground beef
1 envelope taco seasoning mix
10 portobella mushroom caps
10 ounces Cheddar cheese, shredded
1/4 head iceberg lettuce, shredded
1 tomato, chopped
4 to 5 ounces black olives, sliced
5 jalapeño chiles, cut into halves, seeded

Brown the ground beef in a skillet, stirring until crumbly; drain. Stir in the taco seasoning mix. Remove from the heat. Place the mushrooms on a grill rack. Grill until tender, turning frequently. Fill the mushroom caps with the ground beef mixture. Sprinkle with the cheese. Place on a greased baking sheet. Bake at 450 degrees until the cheese melts. Top each with the lettuce, tomato, olives and jalapeño chiles. Serve with desired condiments such as guacamole, sour cream or salsa.

Yield: 10 servings

Gourmet Mushroom Fettuccini

1 (12-ounce) package spinach fettuccini
1 (3-ounce) package sun-dried tomatoes
3 tablespoons extra-virgin olive oil
4 ounces assorted mushrooms
3 garlic cloves, minced
1/2 cup pine nuts

Cook the fettuccini using the package directions; drain. Soften the sun-dried tomatoes in a small amount of hot water in a bowl. Mince the sun-dried tomatoes.

Heat the olive oil in a medium saucepan. Add the mushrooms, sun-dried tomatoes, garlic and pine nuts. Sauté for 2 to 3 minutes or until soft. Remove from the heat. Add to the hot fettuccini and toss to mix.

Yield: 6 servings

Portobella Cremini Stir-Fry

1 1/2 pounds portobella
    mushrooms
2 green bell peppers, cut into
    1/2-inch-thick strips
2 medium onions, cut into
    1/4-inch-thick strips
3 ribs celery, diagonally sliced
1 teaspoon fresh ground ginger
1/4 to 1/2 teaspoon garlic
    powder

1/4 cup vegetable oil
1/2 cup chicken stock
2 tablespoons soy sauce
2 teaspoons cornstarch
2 teaspoons water
8 ounces cremini
    mushrooms, cut into
    1/16-inch-thick slices
Hot cooked rice or
    linguini

Place the portobella mushrooms on a rack in a roasting pan. Roast at 375 degrees for 15 minutes. Remove from the oven and let stand until cool. Cut the mushrooms into 1/4-inch-thick strips.

Sauté the bell peppers, onions, celery, ginger and garlic powder in the oil in a skillet until tender. Add the chicken stock and soy sauce. Simmer for 1 minute. Dissolve the cornstarch in the water in a bowl. Add to the sautéed vegetables. Simmer for 2 to 5 minutes or until thickened, stirring constantly. Add the portobella mushrooms and cremini mushrooms. Simmer for 5 minutes. Serve over hot cooked rice or linguini.

Yield: 3 or 4 servings

PORCINI, OR CÈPE

This full-flavored variety of mushrooms are called porcini in Italy and cèpe in France. Fresh porcini mushrooms are admired for their silken flesh and meaty flavor. Dried porcini mushrooms, the most widely available in the United States, have a smoky, robust flavor that goes a long way.

Tortellini with Shiitake Mushrooms

CHEF ALFRED JACKSON, KENNETT SQUARE INN, KENNETT SQUARE

8 ounces tortellini
4 1/2 ounces shiitake mushrooms
1 teaspoon garlic
1 teaspoon fresh herbs
1/2 cup white wine
1/2 cup cream

Cook the tortellini using the package directions; drain. Sauté the mushrooms, garlic, herbs and wine in a nonstick skillet for 3 minutes. Add the cream gradually, stirring constantly. Cook until thickened to a sauce consistency, stirring constantly. Add the tortellini. Cook until heated through.

Yield: 1 serving

Portobella and Chicken Pasta Casserole

6 ounces sliced portobella mushrooms, cut into thirds
1 tablespoon olive oil
1 pound boneless skinless chicken breasts, cut into 1-inch pieces
1 tablespoon olive oil
1 envelope creamy pesto sauce mix
1 (10-ounce) package frozen peas, thawed, cooked
1 pound penne, cooked, drained

Sauté the mushrooms in 1 tablespoon olive oil in a skillet over medium-high heat for 5 to 6 minutes or until soft. Sauté the chicken in 1 tablespoon olive oil in a skillet until the juices run clear. Prepare the pesto sauce mix using the package directions. Combine the sautéed mushrooms, chicken, peas, pesto sauce and pasta in a large bowl and mix well. Pour into a 9×13-inch baking dish. Bake at 350 degrees for 30 minutes or until bubbly.

Yield: 8 servings

SHIITAKE MUSHROOMS

This large, dark, open-capped mushroom has a full-bodied taste when cooked and has a spongy texture. The mushroom caps are the only part used in food consumption, as the stems are fibrous and tough. Shiitake mushrooms' earthy taste is fabulous when combined with butter, garlic, or chili pepper and when used in recipes calling for sautéing and braising, and in duxelles, sauces, and soups.

Portobella Mushrooms with Chicken

1 pound boneless skinless chicken breasts
1 garlic clove, minced
3 tablespoons olive oil
2 tablespoons dry sherry
6 ounces sliced portobella mushrooms
1 slice prosciutto, chopped (optional)
$1/8$ teaspoon garlic powder
$1/8$ teaspoon oregano
$1/8$ teaspoon salt
$1/8$ teaspoon pepper
2 slices mozzarella cheese

Sauté the chicken and garlic in the olive oil in a skillet until the chicken juices run clear. Add the wine, mushrooms, prosciutto, garlic powder, oregano, salt and pepper. Sauté until the mushrooms are tender. Layer the cheese on top. Cook until the cheese melts.

Yield: 4 servings

Grilled Portobella Neptune

CHEF PETER O'TOOLE, THE GRILLE AT HARTEFELD
NATIONAL GOLF COURSE AND RESTAURANT,
AVONDALE, PENNSYLVANIA

PORTOBELLA MUSHROOMS

Portobella mushrooms have been the big darlings of the food world for the past decade and are now available often at reasonable prices. The stems are usually tough, so it is best to break or slice them off and use to flavor stocks and soups. The caps measure six inches or more in diameter, have a meaty texture and taste, and are great for grilling, simply brushed with a small amount of olive oil.

1 tablespoon chopped white or red onion
1 teaspoon chopped garlic
1 teaspoon chopped shallots
¹/₄ cup red wine
6 tablespoons balsamic vinegar
2 tablespoons lemon juice
¹/₂ teaspoon chopped fresh basil
¹/₂ teaspoon chopped fresh oregano
¹/₄ teaspoon chopped fresh thyme
2 tablespoons olive oil
¹/₄ cup vegetable oil
Salt and pepper to taste
8 large portobella mushroom caps
2 ears of Silver Queen corn, grilled
12 ounces lump crab meat
2 tablespoons butter

Combine the onion, garlic, shallots, wine, balsamic vinegar, lemon juice, basil, oregano, thyme, olive oil, vegetable oil, salt and pepper in a sealable plastic food storage bag and mix well. Add the mushrooms and seal the bag. Marinate in the refrigerator for 2 to 3 hours; drain. Place the mushrooms on a grill rack. Grill for 2 to 3 minutes on each side. Remove from the grill.

Remove the corn kernels from the cobs. Remove any shells from the crab meat. Sauté the corn, crab meat, salt and pepper in the butter in a sauté pan until the crab meat is cooked through. Spoon into the mushroom caps and serve.

Yield: 4 servings

Portobella Mushrooms Stuffed with Shrimp Imperial

HUGO'S INN, KENNETT SQUARE, PENNSYLVANIA

3 eggs
Juice of $1/4$ lemon
$1/2$ cup mayonnaise
1 teaspoon mustard
Salt and pepper to taste
1 pimento, finely chopped, or $1/2$ red bell pepper, finely chopped

$1/2$ green bell pepper, finely chopped
1 pound cooked shrimp, peeled, cut into small pieces
2 slices fresh bread, trimmed, cut into cubes
4 large portobella mushrooms
4 slices cheese

Beat the eggs and lemon juice in a mixing bowl. Add the mayonnaise, mustard, salt and pepper and beat well. Fold in the pimento, green bell pepper, shrimp and bread cubes. Remove the stems from the mushrooms. Place the mushrooms cap side down on a rack in a roasting pan. Roast at 375 degrees for 15 minutes. Place on a baking sheet cap side up. Fill each cap with the shrimp mixture. Top with the cheese. Bake for 15 minutes.

Yield: 4 servings

Portobella Pizza

A CRUSTLESS PIZZA THAT IS LOW IN CARBOHYDRATES.

$1/4$ cup olive oil
3 garlic cloves, chopped
10 portobella mushroom caps
Salt and pepper to taste
$1^1/2$ pounds mozzarella cheese, shredded

20 fresh basil leaves
4 fresh tomatoes, sliced, roasted or grilled
Fresh oregano leaves to taste

Mix the olive oil and garlic in a bowl. Rub on the mushrooms on all sides to coat. Place cap side down in an oiled baking pan. Season with salt and pepper. Alternate the cheese, basil and tomatoes in overlapping slices in a circle on the top of each mushroom cap. Sprinkle with oregano. Add a little water to the baking pan. Bake at 450 degrees until the cheese begins to brown.

Yield: 10 servings

Portobella Sandwiches

CHEF TIM SCHULTZ, THIRD WARD CAFFE, MILWAUKEE, WISCONSIN

1 1/2 teaspoons pesto
1/4 cup mayonnaise
4 portobella mushroom caps
4 (4-inch) focacce
1 cup beef stock or broth
1 tablespoon marsala
1 teaspoon chopped fresh garlic
1/2 teaspoon chopped fresh rosemary
1 1/2 teaspoons extra-virgin olive oil
1 medium beefsteak tomato
1/2 teaspoon chopped fresh basil
1/8 teaspoon sugar
1/8 teaspoon salt
1 large spinach leaf, cut into thin strips

Mix the pesto and mayonnaise in a bowl. Chill in the refrigerator. Place the mushrooms gill side down on a baking sheet. Bake for 8 to 9 minutes. Cut the focacce into halves. Place on a baking sheet. Broil for 2 minutes or until light brown.

Cook the beef stock in a saucepan until reduced to 1/2 cup. Add the wine, garlic, rosemary and olive oil. Bring to a boil. Boil for 1 minute. Add the baked mushrooms to the beef stock mixture and keep warm.

Slice the tomato. Season with basil, sugar and salt. Drain the mushroom caps. Spread the bottom half of each focaccia with the pesto mayonnaise. Layer the spinach, mushrooms and tomato over the pesto mayonnaise. Replace the focaccia tops.

Yield: 4 servings

Dairy AND Eggs

SPONSOR: CHESTER COUNTY DAIRY PROMOTION COMMITTEE

Good pasture and water contribute to successful dairy farming.

Agriculture has been central in the history of Chester County. When Chester County was settled, many people leaving the persecution in Europe brought their cows with them. At that time, 90 percent of the population in Chester County devoted themselves to agriculture. The number has decreased to 2 percent today.

As the towns grew around mills and other agriculture-related businesses, the farmers found making butter was economically feasible. The Sharpless Cream Separator, made in West Chester, met a real need. Nearby Merion Township decided to pass a strict quality control for all milk sold in that township. This led to high-quality milk standards for milk throughout the nation.

Chester County continues to be recognized nationally for agriculture products. The county ranks fifty-sixth in the nation but is the second most threatened by development.

The Chester County Dairy Promotion Committee was formed around 1955. Their mission is to promote the importance of dairy foods in our diets through the dairy princess program. Our former state dairy princess, Charlene Rohrer Ranck, grew up near Russellville. She and her husband Merle have been instrumental in helping promote dairy products. Merle built the dairy barn, which is taken to several events yearly to sell ice cream and milkshakes. Profits from the dairy barn help sponsor teachers attending Agriculture in the Classroom, which promotes agricultural education in the schools. They are also used to fund local dairy promotions.

Dairy promotion has been an important part of our past. As we maintain this program, we are training the next generation to value agriculture.

CLOCKWISE FROM UPPER LEFT: CHROME DAIRY STORE ON BARNSLEY CHROME ROAD IN EAST NOTTINGHAM TOWNSHIP; AMISH USE HORSES TO HARVEST CROPS IN UPPER OXFORD TOWNSHIP; AN AMISH FARMSTEAD ON THE HORSESHOE PIKE IN HONEY BROOK TOWNSHIP.

Hot Artichoke Dip

1 (14-ounce) can non-marinated artichoke hearts, drained
1 cup grated Parmesan cheese
1 cup mayonnaise
Garlic salt to taste
1 pound mozzarella cheese, sliced or shredded

Mash the artichoke hearts in a bowl. Combine the Parmesan cheese and mayonnaise in a bowl and mix well. Layer the mashed artichokes, garlic salt and mozzarella cheese in a baking dish. Spread the Parmesan cheese mixture over the top. Bake at 350 degrees for 20 minutes or until the cheese is melted and bubbly. Serve with melba toast.

Yield: 12 to 20 servings

Hot Pecan Dip

$^1/_2$ cup chopped pecans
2 teaspoons butter
$^1/_4$ teaspoon salt
8 ounces cream cheese, softened
$^1/_2$ cup sour cream
2 teaspoons milk
3 ounces dried beef, finely chopped
1 small onion, grated
$^1/_4$ cup chopped green bell pepper
$^1/_2$ teaspoon garlic salt
$^1/_4$ teaspoon pepper

Place the pecans, butter and salt in a baking pan. Bake at 200 degrees for 15 minutes or until the pecans are toasted. Beat the cream cheese, sour cream and milk in a mixing bowl until smooth. Stir in the beef, onion, bell pepper, garlic salt and pepper. Spread in an 8-inch glass pie plate. Sprinkle with the toasted pecans. Bake at 350 degrees for 20 minutes. Serve hot with crackers or assorted vegetables.

Yield: 12 servings

Cranberry Brie

1 (8-ounce) wheel Brie cheese
1/3 cup whole cranberry sauce
2 tablespoons brown sugar
1/4 teaspoon rum extract or orange extract
1/8 teaspoon nutmeg
2 tablespoons chopped pecans

Peel off the top of the cheese, leaving a 1/4-inch rim. Combine the cranberry sauce, brown sugar, rum extract and nutmeg in a bowl and mix well. Spread over the prepared cheese. Sprinkle with the pecans. Bake at 500 degrees for 4 to 5 minutes or until the cheese is melted. Serve with crackers or sliced green apples.

Yield: 4 servings

Persian Cheese

8 ounces cream cheese, softened
1/2 cup (1 stick) butter, softened
2 scallions with green tops, thinly sliced
1 rib celery, finely chopped
1/4 cup finely chopped green bell pepper
1/2 teaspoon thinly sliced chives
1 tablespoon minced parsley
3/4 teaspoon dillweed

Line a small bowl with plastic wrap. Beat the cream cheese and butter in a mixing bowl until smooth. Add the scallions, celery, bell pepper, chives, parsley and dillweed and mix well. Spoon into the prepared bowl. Chill for 8 to 12 hours. Invert onto a serving plate and remove the plastic wrap. Surround the mold with Triscuits.

Yield: 12 servings

APPLE DIP

Charlene Ranck, Pennsylvania Dairy Princess and Promotion Services Southeast Coordinator, shares this favorite family snack.

Blend 8 ounces cream cheese, 1/2 cup packed brown sugar, 1/2 cup sugar and 1 teaspoon vanilla extract in a food processor until smooth. Spoon into a serving dish. Serve with apple slices. Yield: 1 1/2 cups dip.

Party Cheese Balls

24 ounces cream cheese, softened
8 ounces Roquefort cheese, crumbled, softened
1 (5-ounce) jar Kraft Sharpie cheese
1 teaspoon sugar
$1/2$ teaspoon pepper
2 teaspoons horseradish, drained
1 small onion, grated
Chopped walnuts

Combine the cream cheese, Roquefort cheese, Sharpie cheese, sugar, pepper and horseradish in a bowl and mix well. Stir in the onion. Chill, covered, in the refrigerator. Shape into 4 balls. Roll in chopped walnuts. You may wrap in freezer wrap and store in the freezer.

Yield: 4 cheese balls

Taco Roll-Ups

TIM HENNESSEY, STATE REPRESENTATIVE

12 ounces cream cheese, softened
$^1/_2$ envelope taco seasoning mix
1 (4-ounce) can chopped green chiles, drained
1 (2-ounce) can chopped black and/or green olives, drained
2 tablespoons medium hot salsa, drained
1 (10-count) package soft flour tortillas

Beat the cream cheese and taco seasoning mix in a mixing bowl until smooth. Add the green chiles, olives and salsa and mix well. Spread on the tortillas and roll up. Wrap in plastic wrap. Chill for 8 to 12 hours. Remove the plastic wrap and cut into slices. You may serve with additional salsa.

Yield: 20 servings

Goat Cheese Tarts

6 ounces lean ground beef
1 large onion, chopped
$^1/_4$ cup chopped mushrooms
$^1/_4$ cup finely chopped sun-dried tomatoes
2 tablespoons sour cream
1 tablespoon chopped fresh basil, or 1 teaspoon dried basil
$^1/_2$ teaspoon Worcestershire sauce
1 (1-crust) pie pastry
4 ounces goat cheese or feta cheese
15 pitted black olives, cut into halves or quarters

Brown the ground beef in a medium skillet, stirring until crumbly; drain. Add the onion and mushrooms. Cook until tender. Stir in the sun-dried tomatoes, sour cream, basil and Worcestershire sauce. Roll the pastry $^1/_8$ inch thick on a lightly floured surface. Cut into 2-inch circles. Press into miniature muffin cups. Fill with the ground beef mixture. Top with the cheese and olives. Bake at 425 degrees for 10 minutes or until the pastry is golden brown.

Yield: 15 servings

Quickest-Ever Corn Chowder

1/4 cup chopped onion
1/4 cup (1/2 stick) butter, melted
1/4 cup flour
2 cups milk
2 (16-ounce) cans whole kernel corn
1 (17-ounce) can cream-style corn
2 cups shredded Cheddar cheese (optional)
Salt and pepper to taste

Sauté the onion in the butter in a skillet until translucent. Add the flour and blend well. Stir in the milk gradually. Cook until thickened, stirring constantly. Stir in the undrained whole kernel corn, cream-style corn and cheese. Season with salt and pepper. Cook until the cheese melts.

Yield: 4 to 6 servings

Baked Eggs

8 cups mixed greens (such as mustard, Swiss chard, dandelion and spinach)
1 teaspoon minced garlic
1/8 teaspoon red pepper flakes
3 tablespoons olive oil
1/4 cup water
4 ounces Genoa salami, thinly sliced
8 ounces mozzarella cheese, thinly sliced
6 to 8 eggs
Salt and black pepper to taste

Sauté the mixed greens, garlic and red pepper flakes in the olive oil in a skillet until the greens are wilted. Spread in a greased 10-inch baking dish. Add the water. Arrange the salami and cheese in a circle around the outer edge. Break the eggs 1 at a time into the center. Sprinkle with salt and black pepper. Bake at 450 degrees for 12 to 15 minutes or until the eggs are set and cooked through. You may use thawed frozen mixed greens and omit the 1/4 cup water.

Yield: 6 to 8 servings

Cheese Artichoke Oven Omelet

³/4 cup picante sauce or salsa
1 cup chopped artichoke hearts
¹/4 cup grated Parmesan cheese
1 cup shredded Monterey Jack cheese
1 cup shredded sharp Cheddar cheese
6 eggs
1 cup sour cream

Spread the picante sauce in a buttered 10-inch quiche dish. Arrange the artichokes over the sauce. Sprinkle with the Parmesan cheese, Monterey Jack cheese and Cheddar cheese. Process the eggs in a blender until smooth. Add the sour cream and blend well. Pour over the layers. Bake, uncovered, at 350 degrees for 30 to 40 minutes or until set. Cut into wedges and garnish with tomato wedges and parsley.

Yield: 6 servings

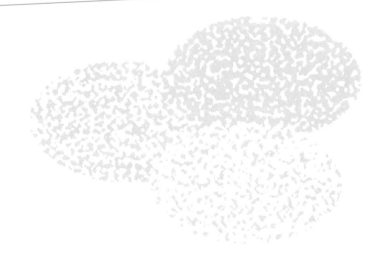

The World's Best Mushroom Omelet

COLIN A. HANNA, CHESTER COUNTY COMMISSIONER

1/4 cup (1/2 stick) butter
1/4 cup sliced shiitake mushrooms
10 to 12 eggs
1 tablespoon chopped chives (optional)
4 slices Velveeta cheese
Jane's Krazy Mixed-up Salt to taste

Melt the butter in a skillet. Add the mushrooms. Simmer, covered, over very low heat for 5 to 10 minutes. Remove to a bowl.

Beat the eggs lightly with a wire whisk in a bowl. Beat in the chives. Pour into the skillet. Spoon the mushrooms and butter in the center of the egg mixture. Cook until the omelet begins to set. Add the cheese and sprinkle with the Mixed-up Salt. Fold the omelet in half. Cook for 30 seconds. Turn the omelet. Cook for 30 seconds longer or until set. Serve immediately.

Yield: 4 servings

Farmers' Casserole

3 cups frozen shredded hash brown potatoes
³/4 cup shredded Monterey Jack cheese with jalapeño chiles, or
   3 ounces shredded Cheddar cheese
1 cup diced cooked ham or Canadian bacon
¹/4 cup sliced green onions
4 eggs, beaten, or 1 cup egg substitute
1 (12-ounce) can evaporated milk
¹/8 teaspoon salt
¹/4 teaspoon pepper

Arrange the potatoes evenly in a greased 2-quart baking dish. Sprinkle with the cheese, ham and green onions. Combine the eggs, evaporated milk, salt and pepper in a bowl and mix well. Pour over the layers. Bake, uncovered, at 350 degrees for 40 to 45 minutes or until the center is set. Let stand for 5 minutes before serving. You may prepare and chill, covered, for 3 to 12 hours. Uncover and bake for 55 to 60 minutes.

   Yield: 6 servings

COWS ARE JUDGED AT THE 1914 WEST CHESTER FAIR.

Tahoe Brunch

YOU CAN GET A HEAD START WITH THIS RECIPE THAT MUST BE PREPARED IN ADVANCE.

1$1/2$ pounds mild Italian sausage
8 ounces mushrooms, sliced
2 cups thinly sliced onions
$1/2$ cup (1 stick) butter
Salt and pepper to taste
12 slices bread
Butter to taste
1 pound Cheddar cheese, grated
5 eggs
2$1/2$ cups milk
1 tablespoon Dijon mustard
1 teaspoon dry mustard
1 teaspoon nutmeg
1 teaspoon salt
$1/8$ teaspoon pepper
Minced fresh parsley to taste

Cook the sausage in a skillet until cooked through; drain. Cut into bite-size pieces. Brown the mushrooms and onions in $1/2$ cup butter in a skillet until tender. Season with salt and pepper to taste. Spread the bread with butter to taste. Layer the buttered bread, mushroom mixture, sausage and cheese $1/2$ at a time in a greased 11×13-inch baking dish. Process the eggs, milk, Dijon mustard, dry mustard, nutmeg, 1 teaspoon salt and $1/8$ teaspoon pepper in a blender until smooth. Pour over the layers. Chill, covered, for 8 to 12 hours. Bake, uncovered, at 350 degrees for 1 hour. Sprinkle with parsley.

Yield: 8 servings

Italian Strata

1 large eggplant
1 tablespoon salt
1 large onion, chopped
8 ounces mushrooms, sliced
2 garlic cloves, minced
2 tablespoons butter, olive oil or bacon drippings
1 pound Italian sausage
6 eggs
2 teaspoons parsley
1 teaspoon oregano
1 teaspoon salt
$1/2$ teaspoon pepper
8 ounces mozzarella cheese, sliced
2 medium tomatoes, sliced
5 ounces Parmesan cheese, grated

Peel the eggplant and cut into $1/2$-inch rounds. Sprinkle with 1 tablespoon salt and place in a colander. Drain for 1 hour. Rinse and pat dry. Place the eggplant on a lightly oiled baking sheet. Broil for 5 minutes per side or until brown.

Sauté the onion, mushrooms and garlic in 2 tablespoons butter in a skillet over medium-high heat for 8 minutes or until soft and just beginning to brown. Remove to a plate.

Crumble the sausage into the skillet. Cook until brown, stirring constantly. Beat the eggs, parsley, oregano, 1 teaspoon salt and pepper in a mixing bowl.

Grease the bottom and side of a 9-inch springform pan generously with butter. Arrange the eggplant in 2 layers in the prepared pan, leaving some space between the slices and cutting the slices to fit the pan; press down. Layer the sautéed vegetables over the eggplant. Place the mozzarella cheese slices over the vegetables. Arrange the tomatoes over the mozzarella cheese in concentric circles. Spread the sausage over the layers. Pour the egg mixture over the top. Sprinkle with Parmesan cheese.

Bake at 375 degrees for 1 hour or until firm, light brown and no liquid is released when pressed lightly in the center. Remove from the oven. Let stand for 10 minutes. Remove the side of the pan. Cut into wedges to serve.

Yield: 4 to 6 servings

French Toast Deluxe

12 to 14 slices bread
8 to 12 ounces cream cheese, softened
1 dozen eggs
2 cups milk
1/2 to 3/4 cup maple syrup
Cinnamon and sugar to taste

Spread 1/2 of the bread with the cream cheese. Top with the remaining bread. Cut each into quarters. Arrange in a single layer in a greased 9×13-inch baking dish. Beat the eggs in a mixing bowl. Add the milk and syrup and beat well. Pour over the top. Chill, covered, for 8 to 12 hours. Uncover and sprinkle with cinnamon and sugar. Bake at 350 degrees for 50 minutes.

Yield: 8 servings

Pizza Rustica

2 egg yolks
1 egg
$^1/_2$ cup (1 stick) butter, softened
1 to 1$^1/_2$ cups flour
Salt and pepper to taste
6 eggs
3 pounds ricotta cheese
4 ounces prosciutto or salami, chopped
Parmesan cheese to taste

Combine 2 egg yolks, 1 egg and butter in a mixing bowl and beat well. Add enough flour to form a soft dough. Season with salt and pepper. Let rest for 1 hour.

Beat 6 eggs in a mixing bowl. Stir in the ricotta cheese. Add the prosciutto, Parmesan cheese, salt and pepper and mix well.

Press the dough into an 11×14-inch baking dish. Add the ricotta cheese mixture. Bake at 350 degrees for 1 hour. You may make extra dough to form a lattice for the top.

Yield: 8 servings

Fontina and Tomato Pie

CHRIS ROSS, STATE REPRESENTATIVE

15 to 20 (1/2-inch-thick) slices focaccia or crusty white bread
2/3 cup dairy milk or soy milk
1 medium red onion, thinly sliced
1 small yellow bell pepper, chopped
2 tablespoons olive oil
Sea salt and pepper to taste
2 cups grated fontina cheese
8 ounces tomatoes, thinly sliced
4 large eggs
1/2 cup grated Parmesan cheese
1 tablespoon chopped fresh oregano

Dip the bread slices into the milk. Line a buttered 9-inch baking dish with the soaked bread, forming a scalloped edge with the crust. Bake at 400 degrees for 15 to 20 minutes or until light golden brown.

Sauté the onion and bell pepper in the olive oil in a medium skillet until soft. Season with sea salt and pepper. Spoon over the bread. Sprinkle with fontina cheese. Cover the top with the tomatoes. Beat the eggs, Parmesan cheese and oregano in a bowl. Pour over the layers. Bake at 400 degrees for 20 to 30 minutes or until the eggs are set.

Yield: 6 servings

Fresh Asparagus Quiche

    1 (1-crust) pie pastry
    3 egg yolks
    2 eggs
    $1/4$ cup sour cream
    1 cup light or heavy cream
    $1/3$ cup milk
    $1/4$ teaspoon grated nutmeg
    1 teaspoon salt
    Freshly ground black pepper to taste
    1 tablespoon minced shallots
    $1^1/_2$ tablespoons butter
    8 ounces fresh asparagus, parboiled, cut into 1-inch pieces
    $2/3$ cup grated Swiss cheese
    $1^1/_2$ tablespoons butter
    $1/8$ teaspoon cayenne pepper

Fit the pastry into a 9-inch pie plate, trimming and fluting the edge. Beat the egg yolks, eggs, sour cream, cream, milk, nutmeg, salt and black pepper in a mixing bowl.

Sauté the shallots in $1^1/_2$ tablespoons butter in a skillet until soft. Add the asparagus. Sauté over high heat for 1 to 2 minutes. Remove from the heat.

Sprinkle $1/2$ of the cheese into the prepared pie plate. Add the asparagus mixture. Sprinkle with the remaining cheese. Pour the egg mixture over the layers, being careful not to overfill. Dot with $1^1/_2$ tablespoons butter. Sprinkle with the cayenne pepper. Bake at 425 degrees for 10 minutes. Reduce the oven temperature to 350 degrees. Bake for 25 to 30 minutes longer or until the top is golden brown and slightly puffed. Serve immediately or at room temperature.

    Yield: 6 servings

Fettuccini Carbonara

> 1 pound fresh spinach fettuccini
> 1 pound sliced bacon
> 1 cup (2 sticks) butter, softened
> 1 cup grated Parmesan cheese
> 6 eggs, lightly beaten
> 2 cups half-and-half
> Salt and pepper to taste

Cook the fettuccini using the package directions; drain. Cook the bacon in a skillet until crisp; drain. Crumble the bacon. Beat the butter and Parmesan cheese in a mixing bowl until blended. Beat in the eggs 1 at a time. Stir in the half-and-half. Pour into a large saucepan. Cook until thickened, stirring constantly; do not boil. Add the fettuccini and toss to coat. Sprinkle with the bacon. Season with salt and pepper. Serve immediately.

Yield: 6 to 8 servings

Skillet Macaroni and Cheese

> 3 tablespoons margarine
> 2 cups uncooked macaroni
> 1/4 cup minced onion
> 2 tablespoons minced green bell pepper
> 1 teaspoon salt
> 1/4 teaspoon dry mustard
> 2 cups water
> 2 cups shredded cheese
> 10 medium sliced olives

Melt the margarine in a skillet. Add the uncooked macaroni, onion, bell pepper, salt and dry mustard. Cook for 5 minutes, stirring frequently. Stir in the water. Bring to a boil. Reduce the heat to low. Simmer, covered, for 10 to 15 minutes or until the macaroni is tender, stirring occasionally. Remove from the heat. Stir in the cheese and olives. Heat until the cheese melts.

Yield: 8 servings

Warm Caramel Apple Bread Pudding

TERRACE RESTAURANT AT LONGWOOD GARDENS

4 cups cream
6 eggs
1/2 cup sugar
1 teaspoon vanilla extract

1 small loaf French bread, cut into
  cubes, toasted
1 pound caramels, melted
2 or 3 Granny Smith apples, sliced

Combine the cream, eggs, sugar and vanilla in a bowl and mix well. Place the bread in a buttered glass baking dish. Alternate layers of the caramels and apples in the prepared dish until full. Pour the cream mixture over the layers. Place the dish in a larger pan. Add enough water to the larger pan to come halfway up the sides of the dish. Bake at 300 degrees for 45 to 60 minutes or until set.

Yield: 8 servings

Bread Pudding

THIS RECIPE FROM MARY KIRK CAN BE TRACED TO ABOUT 1930.

4 eggs
3 cups milk
1 tablespoon vanilla extract
2/3 cup sugar

1/8 teaspoon salt
2 slices bread
Margarine
Nutmeg to taste

Beat the eggs in a mixing bowl. Add the milk, vanilla, sugar and salt and beat well. Pour into a baking dish. Spread the bread with margarine. Cut the bread into quarters. Place on top of the egg mixture. Sprinkle with nutmeg. Place the baking dish in a larger pan. Add enough water to the larger pan to come halfway up the sides of the dish. Bake at 350 degrees for 45 minutes or until a knife inserted in the center comes out clean.

Yield: 4 servings

Rice Pudding

1 1/4 cups uncooked rice
1 1/2 cups sugar
1 (5-ounce) can evaporated milk
1 1/2 cups milk
2 teaspoons vanilla extract
Cinnamon to taste

Combine the rice, sugar and evaporated milk in a large bowl and mix well. Add the milk and vanilla and mix well. Pour into a 3-quart baking dish. Sprinkle with cinnamon. Bake at 350 degrees for 2 hours, stirring 3 times.

Yield: 4 to 6 servings

Lemon Butter

1 cup sugar
3 eggs
3 tablespoons butter
Juice and grated zest of 1 large lemon

Combine the sugar, eggs, butter, lemon juice and lemon zest in a mixing bowl and beat well. Pour into a double boiler. Cook until thickened, stirring constantly. Serve on rolls or crackers or spoon over angel food cake and top with whipped topping. You may pour into a microwave-safe dish and microwave on High for 4 minutes, stirring twice.

Yield: 6 servings

Lime Almond Cheesecake

1/2 cup (1 stick) butter
2 cups finely ground cinnamon graham crackers
1/4 cup sugar
32 ounces cream cheese, softened
1 1/2 cups sugar
1 1/2 tablespoons lime juice
1/8 teaspoon salt
4 large eggs
2 cups sour cream
1/4 cup sugar
1 teaspoon almond extract

Melt the butter in a saucepan over low heat. Process the graham crackers, 1/4 cup sugar and melted butter in a food processor until blended. Press over the bottom and up the side of an ungreased 10-inch springform pan.

Beat the cream cheese and 1 1/2 cups sugar in a mixing bowl for 2 minutes or until soft. Add the lime juice and salt and beat well. Add the eggs 1 at a time, beating at low speed until blended after each addition. Pour into the prepared springform pan. Bake at 350 degrees for 45 minutes. Remove from the oven. Let stand at room temperature for 10 minutes.

Combine the sour cream, 1/4 cup sugar and almond extract in a bowl and mix well using a rubber spatula. Spread evenly over the cheesecake. Return the cheesecake to the oven. Bake for 10 minutes. Remove from the oven and place immediately in the refrigerator to cool to prevent cracks from forming. Serve topped with blueberries, cherries or strawberries if desired.

Yield: 10 to 12 servings

Basic Rules for Cheesecake

1. Add 5 minutes to the baking time if the ingredients are not at room temperature.

2. Place the cheesecake in the refrigerator immediately after baking to prevent cracks.

3. The cheesecake should be baked about 2 days before serving and permitted to mellow in the refrigerator. You may store in the refrigerator uncut and boxed for 7 to 10 days.

4. All cheesecakes except those made of chocolate can be frozen.

5. Never cover the cheesecake with foil or plastic wrap while in the refrigerator. Condensation will cause moisture to collect on the topping of the cheesecake. Cover with a piece of cardboard if the cheesecake is still in the springform pan. Store in a cardboard cake box if the cheesecake has been removed from the pan.

6. Serve the cheesecake on the bottom of the springform pan. The cheesecake should not be moved to another plate.

7. Serve the cheesecake at room temperature.

White Chocolate Cheesecake

KAREN L. MARTYNICK, COUNTY COMMISSIONER

1 1/2 cups chocolate wafer cookie crumbs
1/4 cup sugar
6 tablespoons butter, melted
16 ounces cream cheese, softened
1 cup sugar
1 tablespoon cornstarch
3 eggs, at room temperature
2 tablespoons lemon juice
2 teaspoons vanilla extract
1/8 teaspoon salt
3 cups sour cream
White Chocolate Frosting

Combine the cookie crumbs, 1/4 cup sugar and butter in a bowl and mix well. Press into an 8-inch springform pan. Chill for 30 minutes.

Beat the cream cheese and 1 cup sugar in a mixing bowl until smooth. Beat in the cornstarch. Add the eggs 1 at a time, beating well after each addition. Add the lemon juice, vanilla and salt and beat well. Fold in the sour cream. Pour into the prepared pan.

Place the springform pan on a small baking sheet or on a sheet of heavy-duty foil. Place on the center oven rack. Place another pan filled with 1 inch of boiling water below the springform pan on the bottom oven rack. Bake at 350 degrees for 45 minutes. Turn off oven. Let stand for 1 hour in the oven. Cool in the refrigerator. Cover with a piece of cardboard. Chill for 8 to 12 hours longer.

To serve, remove the side of the springform pan. Reserve 1 cup White Chocolate Frosting. Spread the remaining White Chocolate Frosting over the top and side of the cheesecake. Spoon the reserved White Chocolate Frosting into a pastry bag fitted with a star tip. Pipe stars over the top and around the base of the cheesecake. Serve with fresh raspberries.

Yield: 8 to 10 servings

White Chocolate Frosting

9 ounces imported white chocolate, chopped
12 ounces cream cheese, softened
³/₄ cup (1¹/₂ sticks) unsalted butter, softened
1¹/₂ tablespoons lemon juice

Melt the white chocolate in a double boiler over hot water. Let cool to room temperature. Beat the cream cheese in a mixing bowl until smooth. Add the white chocolate and beat until fluffy. Beat in the butter and lemon juice.

Yield: about 4 cups frosting

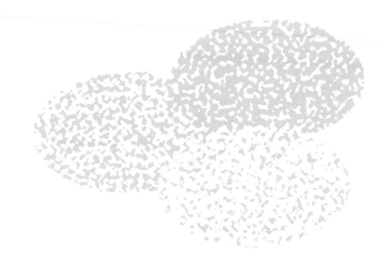

Clementine Cake

1 teaspoon unbleached flour
1 teaspoon superfine sugar
1¾ cups confectioners' sugar
6 egg yolks
Finely grated zest of ½ orange
1 tablespoon Grand Marnier
1 tablespoon orange juice
1 cup unbleached flour, sifted
6 egg whites
¼ teaspoon salt

¾ cup sugar
⅓ cup water
3 tablespoons Grand Marnier
3 cups heavy cream
1 teaspoon orange flower water
5 teaspoons superfine sugar
2 pounds clementines or tangerines, peeled, sectioned
1 cup slivered almonds, toasted

Grease three 9-inch cake pans lightly. Dust with 1 teaspoon flour and 1 teaspoon superfine sugar. Reserve 2 tablespoons of the confectioners' sugar. Beat the remaining confectioners' sugar with the egg yolks in a mixing bowl until thick and pale yellow. Add the orange zest. Add 1 tablespoon Grand Marnier and orange juice gradually, beating constantly. Fold in 1 cup flour.

Beat the egg whites and salt in a mixing bowl until stiff but not dry. Add the reserved confectioners' sugar and beat well. Fold into the batter. Pour into the prepared pans. Bake at 325 degrees for 15 minutes or until the layers test done. Cool in the pans for 5 minutes. Invert onto wire racks to cool completely. Place ¾ cup sugar and water in a saucepan. Cook over low heat until the sugar dissolves, stirring constantly. Boil for 4 to 5 minutes or to 225 degrees on a candy thermometer. Cool the sugar syrup. Stir in 3 tablespoons Grand Marnier.

Whip the cream, orange flower water and 5 teaspoons superfine sugar in a mixing bowl until soft peaks form. Brush the cooled cake layers with the sugar syrup. Pour the remaining syrup over the clementines in a bowl.

To assemble the cake, reserve ⅔ cup of the clementine mixture. Arrange the remaining clementine mixture on 2 of the cake layers. Spread some of the whipped cream over the clementine layers. Stack the cake layers on a cake plate, placing the plain cake layer on top. Spread some of the whipped cream around the side of the cake. Press the almonds on the side. Place the remaining whipped cream in a pastry bag fitted with a rose tip. Arrange the remaining clementine mixture on top of the cake. Pipe whipped cream rosettes on the top.

Yield: 12 servings

Pink Lemonade Cake

1 (2-layer) package yellow cake mix
1 quart vanilla ice cream, softened
6 drops of red food coloring
1 (6-ounce) can frozen pink lemonade concentrate, thawed
1 cup whipping cream
2 tablespoons sugar

Prepare and bake the cake mix using the package directions for two 9-inch cake pans. Remove to wire racks to cool.

Mix the ice cream, red food coloring and 1/2 cup of the lemonade concentrate in a bowl. Spread evenly in a foil-lined 9-inch cake pan. Freeze for 2 to 3 hours or until firm.

Combine the whipping cream, remaining lemonade concentrate and sugar in a bowl. Beat until stiff peaks form.

To assemble, stack 1 cake layer, ice cream layer and remaining cake layer on a cake plate. Spread the whipped cream mixture over the top and side of the cake. Freeze, covered, for 1 to 12 hours.

Yield: 12 servings

Sponge Cake

THIS CAKE WAS ORIGINALLY BAKED IN A WOOD STOVE.

2 cups sifted flour
2 teaspoons baking powder
4 egg yolks
1³/4 cups sugar
³/4 cup warm water
Zest of 1 orange or lemon
1 tablespoon orange or lemon juice
4 egg whites, stiffly beaten

Sift 2 cups sifted flour 5 times. Add the baking powder. Beat the egg yolks and sugar in a mixing bowl for 15 minutes. Add the warm water and mix well. Add the flour mixture a small amount at a time, beating well after each addition. Beat in the orange zest and orange juice. Fold in the stiffly beaten egg whites. Pour into an ungreased 10-inch tube pan. Bake at 350 degrees for 1 hour or until the cake tests done.

Yield: 16 servings

A COZY CHESTER COUNTY KITCHEN.

Triple-Chocolate Truffles

KAREN L. MARTYNICK, COUNTY COMMISSIONER

3/4 cup heavy cream
1/4 cup Cognac
1/4 cup (1/2 stick) butter
8 ounces bittersweet chocolate
8 ounces semisweet chocolate
1/2 cup baking cocoa
1/4 cup confectioners' sugar
Chocolate sprinkles
Chopped nuts

Combine the cream, Cognac, butter, bittersweet chocolate and semisweet chocolate in a heavy saucepan. Cook over very low heat until the chocolate is melted, stirring occasionally. Remove from the heat. Place the saucepan in a larger pan of ice water. Cool until the mixture begins to thicken, stirring constantly. Beat at high speed for 10 to 15 minutes or until the chocolate is very light in color and fluffy.

Shape the chocolate mixture into small balls using 2 teaspoons. Place on a baking sheet lined with waxed paper. Chill until firm.

Sift the baking cocoa and confectioners' sugar into a small bowl. Place the chocolate sprinkles and chopped nuts each in separate bowls. Roll the truffles in 1 of the desired coatings, keeping your hands very cold. You will need to keep a bowl of ice water nearby to dip your hands into periodically. Dry your hands thoroughly before handling the truffles. Return the coated truffles to the baking sheet. Chill in the refrigerator.

Yield: about 2 pounds truffles

SPECIAL MILK PUNCH

Beat 1¹/₂ quarts vanilla ice cream, softened, 3 cups chilled pineapple juice, ¹/₂ cup orange juice, 1 tablespoon lemon juice and 4 cups cold milk in a large mixing bowl until frothy. Pour into a chilled punch bowl. Ladle into punch cups.

Yield: 3 quarts punch

Quickie Bars

Graham crackers
1 cup chopped nuts
1 cup packed brown sugar
1 cup (2 sticks) butter
8 (6-ounce) milk chocolate bars

Line a 10×15-inch baking pan with graham crackers. Sprinkle with the nuts. Combine the brown sugar and butter in a saucepan. Bring to a boil. Boil for 2 minutes or until blended, stirring frequently. Pour over the chopped nuts. Bake at 400 degrees for 6 to 8 minutes. Remove from the oven. Layer the chocolate bars over the top. Let stand until the chocolate is softened. Spread the softened chocolate over the top. Cut into bars immediately.

Yield: 50 servings

Drop Sand Tarts

2 cups (4 sticks) butter, softened
2 cups sugar
3 eggs
4 cups flour
Shredded coconut
Chopped nuts
Cinnamon-sugar

Cream the butter and 2 cups sugar in a mixing bowl until light and fluffy. Add the eggs and beat well. Add the flour gradually, beating constantly. Drop by teaspoonfuls onto ungreased cookie sheets. Press to flatten. Sprinkle with coconut, nuts and cinnamon-sugar. Bake at 375 degrees for 10 minutes. Cool on wire racks.

Yield: 4 dozen cookies

Aunt Helen's Sand Tarts

4 cups flour
1 teaspoon baking soda
1 cup (2 sticks) butter or margarine, softened
1 (1-pound) package confectioners' sugar
3 eggs, beaten
1 teaspoon vanilla extract
1/2 teaspoon nutmeg (optional)

Sift the flour and baking soda together. Beat the butter and confectioners' sugar in a mixing bowl until light and fluffy. Add the eggs, vanilla and nutmeg and beat well. Stir in the flour mixture. Shape into logs and wrap in waxed paper. Chill for 8 to 12 hours. Roll each log into a very thin rectangle on a lightly floured surface. Cut into desired shapes using cookie cutters. Place on cookie sheets. Bake at 350 degrees for 12 minutes. Cool on wire racks.

Yield: 4 dozen cookies

Cranberry Pie

1 1/2 cups gingersnap crumbs
1/2 cup sugar
1/4 cup (1/2 stick) butter, melted
1 quart vanilla ice cream, softened
1 cup whole cranberry sauce

Mix the gingersnap crumbs, sugar and butter in a bowl. Press into a buttered 8- or 9-inch pie plate, packing firmly. Chill in the refrigerator.

Spoon the ice cream into the prepared pie plate. Top with the cranberry sauce. Freeze until firm. Remove from the freezer 20 minutes before serving.

Yield: 8 servings

GUERNSEY COWS IN THEIR FEEDING STALLS AND GRAZING AT
EACHUS DAIRY FARM, WEST CHESTER, AUGUST 1949.

Irresistible Ice Cream Pie

1 pint coffee ice cream, slightly softened
1 (6-ounce) chocolate pie shell
$^3/_4$ cup evaporated milk
$^1/_4$ cup ($^1/_2$ stick) butter
2 ounces unsweetened chocolate
$^1/_2$ cup sugar
$^1/_2$ cup whipping cream
$^1/_4$ cup Kahlúa
$^1/_4$ cup chopped pecans

Spoon the ice cream into the pie shell. Freeze until firm. Combine the evaporated milk, butter, chocolate and sugar in a small saucepan. Cook for 10 to 15 minutes over medium heat until thickened, stirring constantly. Remove from the heat. Cool completely. Spread evenly over the ice cream layer. Freeze until firm.

Beat the whipping cream in a mixing bowl until stiff peaks form. Blend in the liqueur. Spread over the top of the frozen pie. Sprinkle with the pecans. Freeze until firm.

Yield: 8 servings

Lemon Delight Pie

1 (6-ounce) package lemon pudding and pie filling mix
$^1/_2$ cup sugar
$2^1/_4$ cups water
1 egg
1 baked (8-inch) pastry pie shell or graham cracker pie shell
$1^1/_2$ cups whipped topping

Prepare the pie filling using the package directions using $^1/_2$ cup sugar, $2^1/_4$ cups water and 1 egg. Cool for 5 minutes, stirring once or twice. Pour 1 cup of the filling into a bowl. Place plastic wrap directly on the surface. Cool. Pour the remaining pie filling into the pie shell. Chill in the refrigerator.

Stir the reserved filling until smooth. Add the whipped topping and blend well. Spread over the pie. Chill for 3 hours. Garnish with additional whipped topping and lemon slices.

Yield: 8 servings

Lemon Sponge Pie

2 egg whites
1 cup sugar
1 tablespoon butter, softened
2 egg yolks
1 cup milk
Juice and grated zest of 1 lemon
1 tablespoon flour
$^1/_8$ teaspoon salt
1 unbaked (10-inch) pie shell

Beat the egg whites in a mixing bowl until soft peaks form. Add $^1/_4$ cup of the sugar gradually, beating constantly until stiff peaks form.

Combine the remaining sugar, butter, egg yolks, milk, lemon juice, lemon zest, flour and salt in a mixing bowl and beat well. Fold in the stiffly beaten egg whites. Spoon into the pie shell. Bake at 350 degrees for 40 minutes.

Yield: 8 servings

Kiwifruit Lime Pie

3/4 cup sugar
1/3 cup flour
1/8 teaspoon salt
1 3/4 cups milk
3 eggs, beaten
1/4 cup (1/2 stick) butter
2 teaspoons shredded lime peel
1/4 cup lime juice
1 cup lemon yogurt
Few drops of green food coloring
1 (2-crust) pie pastry
1/4 cup apple jelly
Whipped cream
Sliced kiwifruit

Combine the sugar, flour and salt in a saucepan. Stir in the milk. Cook until thickened, stirring constantly. Reduce the heat. Cook for 2 minutes longer. Remove from the heat. Stir 1 cup of the hot mixture into the beaten eggs; stir into the hot mixture. Return to the heat. Cook until thickened, stirring constantly. Do not boil. Remove from the heat. Add the butter, lime peel and lime juice. Fold in the yogurt. Stir in the food coloring. Cover and let stand until cool.

Divide the pastry into 2 equal portions. Roll 1 portion into a circle 1/8 inch thick on a lightly floured surface. Fit into a 9-inch pie plate, trimming and fluting the edge. Bake at 450 degrees for 10 to 12 minutes. Cool. Divide the remaining pastry into 2 equal portions. Roll each portion on a lightly floured surface into an 8-inch circle 1/8 inch thick. Place the circles on a baking sheet. Bake at 450 degrees for 10 minutes. Cool.

To assemble, brush the pastries with the apple jelly. Place 1 cup of the lime filling in the baked pie shell. Cover with one 8-inch pastry circle. Spread with 1/4 cup of the remaining lime filling. Cover with the remaining 8-inch pastry circle. Spread the remaining filling over the top. Chill, covered, for 8 to 12 hours. Just before serving, spread whipped cream over the pie. Arrange the kiwifruit in a decorative pattern over the top.

Yield: 8 servings

Key Lime Pie

CURT SCHRODER, STATE REPRESENTATIVE

6 egg yolks
2 (14-ounce) cans sweetened condensed milk
1 (8-ounce) bottle lime juice concentrate
1 drop of green food coloring
1 (9- to 10-inch) graham cracker pie shell
Whipped topping

Combine the egg yolks and condensed milk in a large mixing bowl and mix well. Stir in the lime juice concentrate and food coloring. Pour into the pie shell. Bake at 350 degrees for 12 minutes. Chill in the refrigerator. Top with whipped topping just before serving.

Yield: 8 servings

Peanut Butter Pie

8 ounces cream cheese, softened
1/2 cup peanut butter
1 cup confectioners' sugar
1/2 cup milk
8 ounces whipped topping
1 (8- or 9-inch) graham cracker pie shell or baked pastry pie shell
1/4 cup finely chopped peanuts

Beat the cream cheese in a mixing bowl until light and fluffy. Add the peanut butter and confectioners' sugar and beat well. Add the milk gradually, beating constantly until blended. Fold in the whipped topping. Spoon into the pie shell. Sprinkle with the peanuts. Freeze until firm.

Yield: 8 servings

HISTORIC GRISTMILLS

Grains Breads AND Pastas

SPONSOR: WILLIAM J. QUINN, INC., FLOUR BROKER

Nature's patchwork quilt can be found in Chester County's fields.
For over three centuries farmers have grown grains in the county's countryside.

As you drive through Chester County in the fall and spring, those bright green fields are wheat—winter wheat. Winter wheat has been a staple of the county since its settlement. Fall is the time to sow winter wheat, which is harvested the following summer. The harvest rush is typically the week after the 4th of July, as trucks brimming with wheat line up for blocks at the mills.

"If it will cover a rabbit by Thanksgiving, you'll have a good crop" has been the saying for years among farmers in this rich land. Winter wheat is a tough crop, able to withstand prolonged spells of dry weather. It is also a good "cash" crop for Chester County farmers.

At one time, Pennsylvania led the country in flour milling. With the advent of a middle purifier, permitting the milling of hard wheat, the milling capital moved to the midwest. Recently, mills have begun moving back to the areas of consumption, with the latest being a 37-million-dollar mill just constructed in Mount Pocono, Pennsylvania.

Chester County and the entire Delaware Valley area are responsible for the huge pretzel industry. The reason it started and flourished here is because Pennsylvania soft red winter wheat is ideal for the manufacture of this delicious product. The majority of the wheat crop is used for pretzel manufacture. When you see those large, bright green fields, think of the generations of Chester County farmers who have thrived on their produce and millions of others who have been nourished by it.

LEFT TO RIGHT: OXFORD GRAIN AND HAY COMPANY IN OXFORD BOROUGH; FEED SACKS AWAIT THE CUSTOMER AT EMBREEVILLE MILL IN NEWLIN TOWNSHIP; THE ENCASED MILLSTONES ARE THE FOCAL POINT IN THE MILL AT ANSELMA IN WEST PIKELAND TOWNSHIP. FIELDSTONE WAS THE PRIMARY BUILDING MATERIAL FOR CHESTER COUNTY'S GRISTMILLS, SUCH AS CAN BE FOUND AT ANSELMA.

Gristmills' Grinding Millstones

Jane L. S. Davidson

Regardless of the culture, grains have been man's daily sustenance for thousands of years. During Chester County's European contact period, the latter seventeenth century and early eighteenth century, Native Americans introduced maize (corn) to the newly arrived immigrants. Gristmills and locally grown grains have contributed to our economic heritage fabric and historic landscape. This stalwart commercial mainstay survived colonial challenges and turmoil; adopted mechanical inventions and nineteenth-century scientific agricultural experimentation; and adapted to agrarian cooperatives, farm consolidations, and technological initiatives.

Grinding grain into flour or animal feed was performed by friction as one round millstone rubbed on top of another. Grinding qualities were achieved by installing stones suitable for desired purposes.

Afterwards, horizontal movement of bolting cloths sifted the flour into various refinements or grades.

Natural resources determined grain yields, gristmill locations, and processing volume. Limestone-enriched sweet soil in the Great Valley between Paoli and Coatesville, combined with abundant rainfall, enhanced grain quality and quantity. Rye was grown on poorer soil instead of wheat. Later, farmers saved rye for their families and shipped wheat and/or flour to Philadelphia for exportation because they could get a better price. Using a waterwheel, the gristmill site needed sufficient operational space for a millpond, headrace, and tailrace, or a combination, near the designated stream. Finally, rushing water descending down the Piedmont hills elevated harnessed waterpower substantially, turning waterwheels faster and faster.

Built of local fieldstone, the gristmill became the community social center as the farmer brought grain to be ground into flour or animal feed and chatted with the miller about the events of the day amidst the clatter of grinding stones, waterwheel, and cogs. Early mills were located in direct ratio to the immigrant and migration settlement patterns as follows:

Francis Chads' in Birmingham, 1710;

Thomas Jerman's in Tredyffrin, 1710;

John Miller's in Avondale, 1714;

Thomas Moore in Downingtown, 1716;

Gayen Stevenson's in Kennett, 1715–16;

Goshen Mill of George Ashbridge in 1717;

Ellis Lewis' in Kennett, 1717;

James Huston's in Birmingham, 1719;

Abiah Taylor's in Bradford, 1719;

Thoms Miller's in Coventry, 1719;

John Jones in Sadsbury, 1721;

Carter, Scott and Willis in East Bradford (now Strode's Mill), 1721; and

Joseph Taylor in Pocopson, 1724.

Founding families combined farming and gristmill operations on their plantations. In 1739 Roger Hunt constructed a three-story merchant mill, 30 by 48 feet of rubble-coursed fieldstone with a Swedish gambrel roof, near the East Branch of the Brandywine Creek in Milltown, now Downingtown Borough. Five years later the Thomas Family, the first settler in West Whiteland Township, erected a "water corn mill." Although the family was Welsh, the composition of the vernacular structure is attributed to a traveling millwright who knew mill construction traditions found in northern England.

Country life excitement of constructing new mills and laying out roads to "mill, to meeting, and to market" was interrupted when England declared war against France. People moved west only to be greeted by the waging conflict through western Pennsylvania's mountainous frontier.

STRODE'S MILL AT THE INTERSECTION OF LENAPE AND BIRMINGHAM ROADS IN 1889.

Colonel Bouquet appointed Roger Hunt Commissary General and charged him with the task of collecting horses, wagons, accoutrements, meat, grains, and flour to create supply wagon trains for Carlisle and various forts.

In 1758 and 1759, Hunt's gristmill business suffered, requiring him to place an ad in the *Pennsylvania Gazette* for a man to run his mill. He struggled to meet Colonel Bouquet's demands and had to broaden his territory into other counties.

Citizens were reluctant to contribute to the cause even when Roger Hunt offered money to pay for the goods. A lack of bags for oats, rye, and flour and township quota shortages compounded his problems, necessitating enlisting additional men to obtain supplies. Credit for barrels of flour from other areas was transferred to Chester County municipalities that could not meet their quotas. In addition to horses, wagons, meats, grains, and flour, Hunt's account books detail the names of men who were responsible for collecting the flour and the wagon train destinations.

BARRELS OF FLOUR	TOWNSHIP	INDIVIDUALS	WAGON TRAIN TRIP
10	E. Bradford	John Vaughn	Carlisle to Ft. Morris
9			Carlisle to Bedford
1			Louden
6	W. Bradford	James Fleming	Ligonier
9	East Caln	Andrew Cox	Carlisle to Bedford
6		John Cox	Bedford to Ligonier
8	West Caln	William Clingan	Fort Bedford
8		Joseph Bishop	Carlisle to Bedford
7	Easttown	Isaac Wayne	Carlisle to Bedford
5		James Wilson	Louden
7			Carlisle to Bedford
6	E. Fallowfield	James Fleming	Bedford to Ligonier
8	W. Fallowfield	Christopher Smith	Carlisle to Bedford
7		Arthur Andrews	Carlisle to Bedford
4		Robert Long	Carlisle to Bedford
6	Kennett	Hugh Wilson	Carlisle to Bedford
9		Michael Kiser	Carlisle to Loudon
6	London Grove	John Farran	Lancaster to Fort Littleton
6	E. Marlborough	Patrick Winter	Lancaster to Fort Littleton
8	W. Marlborough	Hugh Wilson	Carlisle to Bedford
8	E. Nantmeal	Benjamin Evans	Bedford
8	W. Nantmeal	William Noble	Carlisle to Bedford
7		James Grimes	Carlisle to Bedford
8	New Garden	William Bosman	Carlisle to Littleton
6	Newlin	Price and Bosman	Lancaster to Carlisle
8	W. Nottingham	Jacob Varnor	Carlisle to Bedford
7	Thornbury	John Shorts	Carlisle to Bedford
4	Tredyffrin	Joseph Mitchell and John Rowland	Fort Louden to Fort Bedford
8	Westtown	James Erwin	Bedford
8	Whiteland	John Porterfeeld	Carlisle

Samuel Scott paid for flour from his own mill to be shipped to Fort Bedford. Subsequently, Thomas Parke purchased another flour load from Scott for the same location. Finally, in January 1760, Hunt surpassed Colonel Bouquet's quota of sixty-six wagons by twenty-two wagons. Three years later peace arrived, and Roger Hunt returned to farming and milling.

Today the significant historical site in southeastern Pennsylvania is a tranquil setting devoid of the hustle and bustle as shadows dance in the head- and tailraces near the stabilized gristmill ruin and miller's house.

THE ROGER HUNT MILL, CIRCA 1900, ALSO KNOWN AS POLLOCK'S AND RINGWALT'S, IN DOWNINGTOWN WAS A GATHERING LOCATION FOR HORSES AND WAGONS DURING THE FRENCH AND INDIAN WAR.

THE OLD HEADRACE AT ROGER HUNT MILL, DOWNINGTOWN.

Farmers improved their plantations of 150 to 300 acres by continuing to clear an acre per year and increase their crop yields. Stone barns began to replace log barns, and stone merchant gristmills of three and flour stories were erected to accommodate larger milling operations and product volumes for exportation. Mercantile opportunities and expansion lasted only thirteen years before the lifestyle was threatened again.

Contentions escalated between the British and the colonies until war was inevitable. Local farmers, young and old, joined either the Pennsylvania Line or the Chester County Militia. In autumn of 1777, women toiled to bring in the harvest only to find their stores plundered as war came to their doorsteps. That September the British won the Battle of the Brandywine and the surprise attack at Paoli before taking Philadelphia and claiming it as their winter quarters. General George Washington moved his army to Valley Forge and prepared the patriot winter encampment.

Washington issued forage orders to replenish the quickly depleting food and clothing supplies. Between December 1777 and February 1778, William Evans in the Commissary General's office worked with several millers who collected wheat, a precious commodity, to be ground into flour for the troops at Valley Forge. Evans faced obstructions in purchasing wheat for "the want of cash," a cask shortage, and a dishonest forage master.

According to his report filed in February, his efforts yielded 845 barrels of flour from the surrounding gristmills.

BARRELS OF FLOUR	WHERE DEPOSITED	MILES DISTANCE FROM CAMP
40	Crisman's Mill	7
80	Pugh's Mill	12
40	Reed's Mill	14
50	Moore's Mill	16
50	Downing's Mill	16
35	Davis' Mill	25
30	Valentine's Mill	22
76	Hackman's Mill	10
35	Haversack's Mill	23
30	Buffington's Mill	30
100	Miller's Mill	45
16	Cloud's Mill	35
51	Evans' Mill	50
52	Reynold's Mill	50
40	Linker's Mill	50
30	McEvans' Mill	45
64	Alexander's Mill	45

Although the conflict moved elsewhere, Chester County families suffered for years, even after the end of the Revolutionary War in 1782. Gradually, renewed fields yielded crops to turn the waterwheels.

Soon, wheelwrights, blacksmiths, tavern keepers, and itinerant weavers joined gristmill hubs, which in turn expanded the local economy. Others took advantage of increasing population centers and new roads to begin new business ventures.

In 1793 Michael Gunkel, an astute businessman, built his first gristmill, Spring Mill, on the Conestoga Road, now Route 401 near Route 202, in the fertile Great Valley. Constructed of white oak beams and posts and rubble fieldstone, the mill had an operation capacity of eighteen hours a day at the peak of its productivity. This important East Whiteland Township historical icon has been restored, and local citizens have come together to further enhance its significance through heritage interpretation.

THE MILL AT ANSELMA, ALSO KNOWN AS THE SAMUEL LIGHTFOOT MILL, ON THE CONESTOGA ROAD, ROUTE 401, IN WEST PIKELAND TOWNSHIP.

Earlier, Samuel Lightfoot had erected a gristmill upcountry on the same road on Pickering Creek. Three generations of the Lightfoot family operated the mill before selling it to Lewis Rees and James Benson in 1812. A succession of owners overlaid nineteenth-century inventions and twentieth-century innovations on the eighteenth-century wooden works.

Of these additions, the introduction of Oliver Evans' "automatic" milling inventions to the Mill at Anselma is noteworthy. Oliver E. Collins, the most recent miller, recognized the declining gristmill business and, using country ingenuity, he operated a sawmill, a cider press, metalworking machinery, and the Anselma Post Office to support his family.

According to Stephen J. Kindig, historic milling consultant, "The Mill Anselma, and its collections of machinery, is remarkable and unique on a variety of levels. Simply stated, I have never found an example to equal this Mill. Whereas there are several partial examples extant, the Mill at Anselma is the only one complete in all the necessary machinery—of the 'Wooden Age'—to produce 'white flour' from wheat and animal feed from various other grains."

WOOD GEARING IN THE MILL AT ANSELMA, WEST PIKELAND TOWNSHIP.

GEARINGS IN THE MILL AT ANSELMA, WEST PIKELAND TOWNSHIP.

GRAIN CHUTE IN THE
MILL AT ANSELMA,
WEST PIKELAND TOWNSHIP.

Last year the French and Pickering Creeks Conservation Trust, who had acquired The Mill at Anselma in 1982, conveyed ownership to The Mill at Anselma Preservation and Educational Trust, Inc. The latter organization has initiated efforts to restore and operate the millworks for heritage interpretation purposes.

A HINT OF SPRING ARRIVES AT
GRUBBS MILL IN EAST BRADFORD
TOWNSHIP, MARCH 1935.

IN 1922, EARL J. ESSICK
PHOTOGRAPHED THE CHRISTMAN-
WETZLER GRISTMILL IN SOUTH
COVENTRY TOWNSHIP.

The proliferation of railroads and canals during the nineteenth century influenced Chester County's agricultural economy. The gristmilling operations shifted from southeastern Pennsylvania to Rochester, New York, and then moved to the Midwest. By 1880 only two of the 264 gristmills in Chester County ground grains for export.

HARVESTING WHEAT WITH A
HORSE-DRAWN BINDER.

GILBERT'S MILL IN 1936,
FORMERLY KNOWN AS TAYLOR'S MILL,
NORTH OF WEST CHESTER ON ROUTE 100,
WEST GOSHEN TOWNSHIP.

The miller had to be satisfied with custom milling for his neighbors. Farmers had tin templates with their names and sometimes the year, which were painted on sacks as grain was being ground. Former grainfields became pastures for dairy cows because the farmer took advantage of the expanding markets via railroad to ship butter, eggs, cheese, and milk to Philadelphia.

THE RACEWAY SUPPLIES WATER AT GILBERT'S MILL, WEST GROVE, TO TURN ITS WATERWHEEL, CIRCA 1900.

IN 1911 THE LLOYD FAMILY HARVESTED THEIR WHEAT ON VALLEY BROOK FARM IN CALN TOWNSHIP.

As suburbia replaced fields in eastern Chester County in the twentieth century, farmers continued to harvest wheat and other grains in northern, central, southern, and western sections. Today one-third of the county's acreage still sustains the agricultural economy. But the rushing waters on the overshot waterwheel, the clatter of cogs, grinding millstones, the dragonfly buzzing over the headrace, and the chatter of mill voices are silent. Some gristmill structures still stand as sentinels in their communities as homes and businesses. Initiatives have also begun to interpret the contributions that gristmills have given to Chester County's agricultural economic heritage for more than three centuries.

CUPOLA MILL AND FOUNDRY IN HONEY BROOK TOWNSHIP
AS IT APPEARED IN 1948.

Chilled Oriental Pasta with Shrimp

12 ounces fresh snow peas, trimmed
1 pound shrimp, peeled, deveined
16 ounces angel hair pasta
2 cups grated carrots
1/2 cup thinly sliced green onions
2 tablespoons sesame seeds, toasted
1 piece gingerroot (the size of a quarter), grated

3 small kiwifruit, peeled, chopped
4 teaspoons fresh lime juice
2 teaspoons vegetable oil
1 teaspoon oriental sesame oil
3 tablespoons orange juice
1 tablespoon honey
1/4 teaspoon salt

Blanch the snow peas in boiling water in a large saucepan for 2 minutes. Remove the snow peas to a colander using a slotted spoon. Rinse immediately with cold water; drain. Add the shrimp to the boiling water. Cook until the shrimp turn pink. Remove the shrimp to a bowl using a slotted spoon. Add the pasta to the boiling water. Cook until the pasta is al dente. Drain and rinse with cold running water. Drain well. Combine the pasta, snow peas, shrimp, carrots, green onions and sesame seeds in a large bowl. Combine the gingerroot, kiwifruit, lime juice, vegetable oil, sesame oil, orange juice, honey and salt in a bowl and blend well. Pour over the pasta mixture and toss to mix. Chill, covered, until serving time.

Yield: 8 servings

Greek Pasta Salad with Shrimp

8 ounces orzo, cooked
2 cups chopped peeled cooked shrimp
1 medium cucumber, chopped
4 ounces feta cheese, crumbled
1/2 cup chopped black olives
1/2 cup chopped green olives
2 large tomatoes, chopped

1/4 cup olive oil
1 tablespoon chopped fresh parsley
1 garlic clove, minced
1 tablespoon oregano
1/2 teaspoon salt
1/2 teaspoon pepper
1/4 cup white vinegar

Combine the pasta, shrimp, cucumber, feta cheese, black olives, green olives, tomatoes and olive oil in a large bowl and toss to mix. Combine the parsley, garlic, oregano, salt, pepper and vinegar in a bowl and mix well. Pour over the orzo mixture and toss to coat. Chill, covered, for 1 to 24 hours.

Yield: 8 servings

Tortellini Soup with Ham and Zucchini

2 (14-ounce) cans chicken broth
1 1/2 cups water
4 ounces cheese tortellini
4 ounces cooked ham, cut into 1/2-inch
   cubes

1 medium zucchini, cut into
   1/2-inch cubes

Bring the chicken broth and water to a boil in a saucepan over medium-high heat. Add the tortellini. Cook for 4 minutes. Add the ham and zucchini. Cook for 2 to 3 minutes longer or until the pasta is al dente.

Yield: 4 servings

Vegetable Broccoli Lasagna

2 (10-ounce) cans cream of broccoli soup
1 (10-ounce) package frozen chopped
   broccoli
3 carrots, thinly sliced
1 large onion, chopped
1 tablespoon vegetable oil
1/4 cup water

3 tablespoons vegetable oil
12 ounces mushrooms, sliced
4 cups shredded mozzarella cheese
15 ounces ricotta cheese
2 eggs
12 lasagna noodles, cooked, drained

Heat the soup and broccoli in a 2-quart saucepan until the broccoli is thawed. Sauté the carrots and onion in 1 tablespoon vegetable oil in a 10-inch skillet over medium heat until light brown. Reduce the heat to low. Stir in the water. Simmer, covered, for 15 minutes or until the vegetables are tender. Pour into a bowl. Add 3 tablespoons vegetable oil to the skillet and heat over high heat. Add the mushrooms. Sauté until light brown and the liquid is evaporated. Remove from the heat. Add the carrot mixture and mix well. Mix the mozzarella cheese, ricotta cheese and eggs in a bowl.

Spread 1 cup of the broccoli sauce in a 9×13-inch baking dish. Layer 1/2 of the noodles, 1/2 of the cheese mixture, all the carrot mixture and 1/2 of the remaining broccoli sauce in the prepared dish. Top with the remaining noodles, cheese mixture and broccoli sauce. Bake at 375 degrees for 45 minutes or until bubbly. Let stand for 10 minutes before serving.

Yield: 10 servings

Pasta with Mushrooms, Asparagus and Sun-Dried Tomatoes

3 garlic cloves, minced
2 tablespoons olive oil
2 cups sliced mixed wild mushrooms (such
  as cremini and shiitake mushrooms) or
  button mushrooms
8 ounces asparagus, cut into 1-inch pieces
1/2 cup sun-dried tomatoes, cut into thin
  strips
1/2 cup dry white wine

1/2 cup heavy cream or half-and-half
1/4 cup mascarpone cheese or
  cream cheese
1 tablespoon chopped fresh parsley
Salt and pepper to taste
12 ounces fusilli or other spiral pasta,
  cooked, drained
1/4 cup freshly grated Parmesan cheese

Sauté the garlic in the hot olive oil in a large heavy skillet over medium-high heat for
1 minute or until golden brown. Add the mushrooms, asparagus and sun-dried tomatoes.
Sauté for 10 minutes or until tender and most of the liquid has evaporated. Add the wine.
Boil for 3 minutes or until the liquid is reduced by 1/2. Add the cream, mascarpone cheese
and parsley. Simmer for 8 minutes or until the liquid is reduced to a sauce consistency.
Season with salt and pepper. Remove from the heat. Pour over the hot cooked pasta in
a large bowl and toss to coat. Sprinkle with the Parmesan cheese. You may add chopped
cooked chicken if desired.

Yield: 6 servings

Macaroni and Cheese

2 cups elbow macaroni, cooked,
  drained
Bacon bits to taste
Sliced tomatoes (optional)

16 ounces Cheddar cheese, cut into
  1/4-inch slices
Vegetable oil
1/4 cup milk

Place 1/2 of the macaroni in a greased 2-quart baking dish. Layer with bacon bits, tomato
slices and 1/2 of the cheese. Add the remaining macaroni. Arrange the remaining cheese
over the top. Brush with vegetable oil. Pour the milk over the layers. Bake at 350 degrees
for 30 minutes.

Yield: 6 to 8 servings

Pumpkin Risotto

1/4 cup olive oil
1 3/4 cups uncooked arborio rice
1 1/2 cups 1/2-inch cubes fresh pumpkin
  or squash
1/2 cup white wine

6 to 7 cups Pumpkin Broth
1 tablespoon fresh sage
2 cups arugula, chopped
1/3 cup shredded mozzarella cheese
Salt and pepper to taste

Heat the olive oil in a 3-quart saucepan. Add the rice and pumpkin and toss to coat. Add the wine, stirring until absorbed. Add 1/2 cup of the warm Pumpkin Broth, stirring constantly. Cook until the liquid is absorbed, stirring constantly. Repeat the process with the remaining Pumpkin Broth until all of the broth has been absorbed and the rice is soft. The total cooking time for the rice will be about 20 to 25 minutes. Stir in the sage, arugula, cheese, salt and pepper. Serve immediately.

Yield: 6 servings

Pumpkin Broth

1 tablespoon butter
1 medium onion, thinly sliced
2 carrots, thinly sliced
1 rib celery, thinly sliced
1 leek (white and light green portions
  only), thinly sliced
2 cups canned pumpkin

8 cups chicken broth
1/2 teaspoon black peppercorns
4 allspice berries
1/4 teaspoon nutmeg
1/4 stick cinnamon
2 tablespoons maple syrup

Melt the butter in a large stockpot. Add the onion, carrots, celery and leek. Cook for 10 minutes or until tender. Add the pumpkin. Cook for 2 to 3 minutes. Add the chicken broth, peppercorns, allspice, nutmeg, cinnamon and maple syrup. Simmer for 45 minutes. Strain the broth and keep warm.

Yield: 10 cups broth

Southern Buttermilk Biscuits

2 cups flour
1 teaspoon salt
2 teaspoons baking powder
$^1/_3$ teaspoon baking soda
$^1/_2$ cup shortening
$^2/_3$ cup buttermilk

Sift the flour, salt, baking powder and baking soda into a bowl. Cut in the shortening until crumbly. Create a well in the center and add the buttermilk. Stir to form a soft dough. Knead on a lightly floured surface until smooth. Roll the dough $^1/_2$ inch thick. Cut the dough into circles using a lightly floured biscuit cutter. Place on a greased baking sheet. Bake at 450 degrees for 10 to 12 minutes or until light brown.

Yield: 1 dozen biscuits

HARVESTING WHEAT AT "HILL TOP" FARM OF
A. B. HUEY, POCOPSON TOWNSHIP, ON JULY 10, 1940.

Cranberry Orange Scones

2 cups flour
2 tablespoons plus 1 teaspoon
 sugar
1 tablespoon orange zest
2 teaspoons baking powder
$1/2$ teaspoon salt
$1/4$ teaspoon baking soda
$1/2$ cup (1 stick) butter
$1/2$ cup dried cranberries
$1/4$ cup orange juice
$1/4$ cup half-and-half

1 egg
1 tablespoon milk
1 tablespoon sugar
$1/2$ cup confectioners'
 sugar
1 tablespoon orange juice
$1/2$ cup (1 stick) butter,
 softened
2 to 3 tablespoons orange
 marmalade

Mix the flour, 2 tablespoons plus 1 teaspoon sugar, orange zest, baking powder, salt and baking soda in a bowl. Cut in $1/2$ cup butter until crumbly. Combine the cranberries, $1/4$ cup orange juice, half-and-half and egg in a small bowl and mix well. Add to the flour mixture and stir to form a soft dough. Knead gently 6 to 8 times on a floured surface. Do not over knead. Pat the dough into an 8-inch circle. Cut into 10 wedges. Place the wedges on an ungreased baking sheet. Brush with the milk. Sprinkle with 1 tablespoon sugar. Bake at 400 degrees for 12 to 15 minutes or until light brown.

Mix the confectioners' sugar and 1 tablespoon orange juice in a bowl until smooth. Drizzle over the hot scones. Serve with a mixture of $1/2$ cup butter and orange marmalade.

Yield: 10 scones

BASIC PASTRY

Mix 2 cups flour and $1/2$ teaspoon salt in a bowl. Cut in $2/3$ cup shortening until crumbly. Stir in 4 to 5 tablespoons water to form a soft dough. Shape into a ball. Divide the dough into 2 equal portions. Roll into 2 circles. Fit into two 8- or 9-inch pie plates, or use to make a 2-crust pie.

Makes 2 pie pastries

Pumpkin Scones with Maple Butter

1 1/2 cups unbleached flour
1/2 cup whole wheat flour
3 tablespoons dark brown sugar
2 teaspoons baking powder
1/2 teaspoon baking soda
1/2 teaspoon salt
1 1/2 teaspoons apple pie spice
6 tablespoons unsalted butter,
   cut into pieces

1/3 cup finely chopped dried apples
1/3 cup currants
1 large egg
1/4 cup buttermilk
1/2 cup canned pumpkin purée
2 tablespoons half-and-half or milk
2 tablespoons sugar
Maple Butter

Mix the unbleached flour, whole wheat flour, brown sugar, baking powder, baking soda, salt and apple pie spice in a medium bowl. Cut in 6 tablespoons butter until crumbly. Add the dried apples and currants. Mix the egg, buttermilk and pumpkin purée in a small bowl. Add to the flour mixture and stir to form a sticky dough. Knead 8 times or until the dough holds together on a lightly floured surface. Divide the dough into 2 equal portions. Pat each portion into a circle 1 inch thick and about 6 inches in diameter. Cut each circle into quarters, forming wedges.

Place the wedges about 1 inch apart on a baking sheet lined with parchment paper. Brush the tops with the half-and-half. Sprinkle with 2 tablespoons sugar. Bake at 400 degrees for 15 to 20 minutes or until crusty and golden brown. Serve immediately with Maple Butter. You may cool on a wire rack and freeze in heavy-duty freezer bags for up to 1 month.

Yield: 8 scones

Maple Butter

1/2 cup (1 stick) unsalted butter, softened
3 tablespoons maple syrup

Cream the butter and maple syrup in a small bowl until fluffy. Store, covered, in the refrigerator for up to 3 days. Bring to room temperature before serving.

Yield: 1/2 cup maple butter

Mashed Potato Doughnuts

4 cups flour
1 tablespoon baking powder
$^1/_4$ teaspoon salt
$^1/_8$ teaspoon nutmeg
1 cup mashed cooked potatoes
1 cup sugar
2 eggs

2 tablespoons butter, softened
1 teaspoon vanilla extract
$^1/_2$ cup milk
Vegetable oil for deep-frying
$^1/_2$ cup sugar
1 to 2 teaspoons cinnamon

Mix the flour, baking powder, salt and nutmeg together. Beat the mashed potatoes and
1 cup sugar in a mixing bowl. Add the eggs, butter, vanilla and milk and beat well. Stir in
the flour mixture to form a soft dough. Roll into a circle on a lightly floured surface. Cut
with a doughnut cutter. Deep-fry in 375-degree oil in a deep fryer until brown, turning
once. Drain on paper towels. Mix $^1/_2$ cup sugar and cinnamon in a plastic food storage bag.
Add the warm doughnuts and shake to coat.

Yield: 40 doughnuts

Banana French Toast

2 ripe medium bananas, sliced $^1/_4$ inch
    thick
1 tablespoon lemon juice
12 ($^1/_2$-inch-thick) untrimmed slices
    French bread
$^1/_2$ cup semisweet or milk chocolate chips
2 eggs, beaten

$^3/_4$ cup milk
2 tablespoons honey
$^1/_2$ teaspoon vanilla extract
$^1/_4$ teaspoon cinnamon
$^1/_4$ cup sliced almonds
1 teaspoon sugar
Maple syrup

Toss the bananas gently with the lemon juice in a bowl. Arrange $^1/_2$ of the bread slices in a
greased 2-quart square baking dish. Layer the bananas, chocolate chips and remaining bread
slices in the prepared dish. Combine the eggs, milk, honey, vanilla and cinnamon in a bowl
and beat well. Pour over the layers gradually to coat evenly. Chill, covered, for 6 to 24 hours.
Uncover the baking dish. Sprinkle the top with almonds and sugar. Bake at 425 degrees for
5 minutes. Reduce the oven temperature to 325 degrees. Bake for 20 to 25 minutes longer
or until a knife inserted near the center comes out clean and the top of the French toast is
light brown. Let stand for 10 minutes. Serve with maple syrup.

Yield: 4 servings

CORNMEAL MUSH PANCAKES

Cornmeal is used in many parts of the world in much the way we use bread or potatoes. Italy's polenta and Romania's mamaliga are cooked cornmeal served with sauces or meats.

Mix 1/4 cup cornmeal and 1/4 cup cold water in a medium microwave-safe bowl. Season with salt to taste. Stir in 3/4 cup boiling water. Microwave for 1 1/2 minutes or until the mixture boils. Spoon a small amount at a time on a hot greased griddle. Cook until brown on both sides, turning once. Serve with syrup, jelly or honey.

Apple Walnut Pancakes

COLIN A. HANNA, COMMISSIONER

Pancake mix
3 or 4 tablespoons frozen
    Granny Smith apple juice
    concentrate

1 cup finely chopped
    peeled apples
3/4 cup chopped walnuts

Prepare the pancake mix using the package directions for a 4-serving size of pancakes and adding a smaller amount of milk so that the mix is rather thick. Add apple juice concentrate, apples and walnuts and mix until evenly distributed. The mixture should be the consistency of pancake batter.

Pour 1/4 cup at a time on a lightly greased griddle over medium heat. Cook until bubbles appear on the surface and the underside is golden brown. Turn the pancake. Cook until golden brown on the bottom.

Yield: 4 servings

Zucchini Pancakes

1/3 cup baking mix
1/2 cup shredded Cheddar
    cheese
Freshly ground pepper to taste

Fresh or dried herbs to
    taste
3 eggs, beaten
2 cups shredded zucchini

Mix the baking mix, Cheddar cheese, pepper and herbs in a bowl. Add the eggs and mix well. Stir in the zucchini. Spoon a small amount at a time onto a hot greased griddle. Cook until bubbles appear on the surface and the underside is golden brown. Turn the pancake. Cook until golden brown on the bottom. Serve hot or cold.

Yield: 4 servings

Once-a-Week Waffle Mix

1 1/3 cups quick-cooking oats
1/2 cup whole wheat flour
2 1/2 teaspoons baking powder
1 teaspoon baking soda
3/4 teaspoon salt
1/4 cup butter-flavor shortening or vegetable oil
2 1/2 cups all-purpose or unbleached flour

Process the oats, whole wheat flour, baking powder, baking soda and salt in a food processor until the oats are ground to a powder. Add the shortening, processing constantly. Pulse for 1 minute or until the shortening is evenly incorporated, stopping to scrape down the side of the bowl as needed. Add the all-purpose flour. Continue to pulse until mixed. Place in a jar or a sealable plastic food storage bag. Shake or stir once before storing to aerate the mix slightly. Seal and store in the refrigerator for up to 1 month.

For waffles, combine 1/2 cup of the waffle mix with 1 egg and 1/4 cup buttermilk and stir until smooth. Cook in a waffle iron using the manufacturer's instructions. You may use the mix for pancakes by increasing the amount of buttermilk to 1 cup.

Yield: 4 1/2 cups mix

Favorite Waffles

2 egg whites
2 cups milk
2 egg yolks
1/3 cup vegetable oil
1/2 teaspoon vanilla extract
2 cups flour
1 tablespoon baking powder
1/2 teaspoon salt

Beat the egg whites in a mixing bowl until stiff peaks form. Combine the milk, egg yolks, oil and vanilla in a bowl and beat well. Stir in the flour, baking powder and salt. Fold in the stiffly beaten egg whites. Cook in a waffle iron using the manufacturer's instructions.

Yield: 8 servings

Oatmeal Applesauce Bread

1¹/₂ cups rolled oats
¹/₂ cup all-purpose flour
¹/₂ cup whole wheat flour
¹/₂ cup packed brown sugar
¹/₄ cup bran
1 teaspoon baking soda
1 teaspoon baking powder

1 teaspoon cinnamon
¹/₂ teaspoon salt
1 cup applesauce
¹/₃ cup vegetable oil
2 eggs
1 cup raisins
¹/₂ cup chopped black walnuts

Mix the oats, all-purpose flour, whole wheat flour, brown sugar, bran, baking soda, baking powder, cinnamon and salt in a large bowl. Add the applesauce, oil and eggs and stir until blended. Stir in the raisins and walnuts. Pour into a greased and floured nonstick 5×9-inch loaf pan. Bake at 350 degrees for 50 to 60 minutes or until a wooden pick inserted in the center comes out clean. Cool in the pan for 10 minutes. Invert onto a wire rack to cool completely. Serve the next day for enhanced flavor.

Yield: 12 servings

Pumpkin Bread

4 eggs, beaten
2 cups sugar
1 cup vegetable oil
2 cups mashed cooked pumpkin
3¹/₂ cups flour
1 teaspoon baking powder
2 teaspoons baking soda

¹/₂ teaspoon salt
2 teaspoons cinnamon
¹/₂ teaspoon nutmeg (optional)
¹/₂ teaspoon allspice (optional)
²/₃ cup water
1 cup raisins
1 cup chopped nuts

Combine the eggs, sugar, oil and pumpkin in a large mixing bowl and mix well. Add the flour, baking powder, baking soda, salt, cinnamon, nutmeg and allspice and mix well. Add the water and mix well. Stir in the raisins and nuts. Pour into 2 greased and floured 5×9-inch loaf pans. Bake at 350 degrees for 45 to 50 minutes or until a knife inserted in the centers comes out clean.

Yield: 2 loaves

Blueberry Nut Muffins

1¹/₂ cups blueberries
2 tablespoons flour
¹/₂ cup sugar
¹/₂ cup vegetable oil
1 egg
1¹/₂ cups flour

2 teaspoons baking powder
¹/₂ teaspoon baking soda
¹/₂ teaspoon salt
¹/₂ cup sour milk or buttermilk
¹/₂ cup nuts

Combine the blueberries and 2 tablespoons flour in a small bowl and toss to coat. Beat the sugar, oil and egg in a mixing bowl. Add 1¹/₂ cups flour, baking powder, baking soda and salt and mix well. Stir in the sour milk. Fold in the blueberries and nuts. Pour into greased muffin cups, filling ¹/₂ full. Bake at 400 degrees for 20 minutes.

Yield: 1 dozen muffins

Streusel-Topped Berry Muffins

1¹/₂ cups flour
¹/₂ cup sugar
2 teaspoons baking powder
¹/₄ teaspoon baking soda
¹/₄ teaspoon salt
1 large egg
1 cup sour cream

¹/₄ cup (¹/₂ stick) butter, melted
1 cup berries
¹/₂ cup chopped walnuts or pecans
¹/₄ cup flour
2 tablespoons butter, softened
¹/₂ teaspoon cinnamon

Mix 1¹/₂ cups flour, sugar, baking powder, baking soda and salt in a large bowl. Beat the egg, sour cream and ¹/₄ cup butter in a mixing bowl. Add to the flour mixture and stir until moistened. Fold in the berries. Spoon into 12 muffin cups lined with paper liners.

Combine the walnuts, ¹/₄ cup flour, 2 tablespoons butter and cinnamon in a bowl and mix with your finger until crumbly. Spoon about 2 teaspoons of the topping onto each muffin. Bake at 375 degrees for 20 to 25 minutes or until a wooden pick inserted in the centers comes out clean. Cool for 1 hour before serving. You may add 2 tablespoons brown sugar to the topping if desired.

Yield: 1 dozen muffins

Philadelphia Sticky Buns

1 cake compressed yeast, or
   1 envelope dry yeast
1/4 cup lukewarm water
1 cup scalded milk
1/4 cup shortening
1/4 cup sugar
1 teaspoon salt
3 1/4 to 3 1/2 cups sifted flour
1 egg, beaten

1/4 cup (1/2 stick) butter, melted
1/2 cup packed brown sugar
2 teaspoons cinnamon
1 cup packed brown sugar
1/2 cup (1 stick) butter
1 tablespoon light corn syrup
Chopped pecans (optional)
Raisins or currants (optional)
2 teaspoons water

Soften the yeast in 1/4 cup lukewarm water. Combine the scalded milk, shortening, sugar and salt in a mixing bowl and mix well. Cool to lukewarm. Add 1 cup of the flour and beat well. Add the yeast and egg and beat well. Remove 1 beater. Add enough of the remaining flour gradually to form a soft dough, beating well after each addition. Cover and let rise for 1 1/2 to 2 hours or until doubled in bulk. Punch the dough down. Divide the dough into 2 equal portions. Roll each into an 8×13-inch rectangle on a floured surface. Brush the rectangles with 1/4 cup melted butter. Mix 1/2 cup brown sugar and 2 teaspoons cinnamon in a bowl. Sprinkle over each rectangle. Roll each rectangle as for a jellyroll, pressing the ends to seal. Cut each into 9 slices.

Mix 1 cup brown sugar, 1/2 cup butter and corn syrup in a bowl. Add pecans and raisins. Divide between 2 baking pans. Add 1 teaspoon water to each pan. Melt over low heat. Remove from the heat.

Arrange 9 slices of dough in each baking pan. Let rise for 35 to 45 minutes or until doubled in bulk. Bake at 375 degrees for 25 minutes. Cool for 1 to 2 minutes. Invert onto foil or a serving plate. Let stand until cool. You may freeze the sticky buns if desired.

Yield: 18 sticky buns

Cinnamon Buns

Chopped nuts
Raisins
1 (25-ounce) package frozen rolls
1/2 cup packed brown sugar

1 (6-ounce) package vanilla pudding
  and pie filling mix
1 teaspoon cinnamon
1/2 cup (1 stick) margarine, melted

Sprinkle nuts and raisins in a 1-piece tube pan or a 9×13-inch baking pan. Arrange the frozen rolls in the prepared pan. Mix the brown sugar, pudding mix and cinnamon in a bowl. Sprinkle over the rolls. Pour the melted margarine over the top. Cover with plastic wrap. Let rise for 8 to 12 hours. Bake, uncovered, at 350 degrees for 35 minutes. Remove from the pan.

Yield: 24 servings

White Bread

2 envelopes dry yeast
3/4 cup warm (105 to 115 degrees)
  water
1/4 cup sugar
1 tablespoon salt

2 2/3 cups warm (105 to 115 degrees)
  water
3 tablespoons shortening
9 to 10 cups flour
Butter or margarine, softened

Dissolve the yeast in 3/4 cup warm water in a large bowl. Add the sugar, salt, 2 2/3 cups warm water, shortening and 5 cups of the flour and beat until smooth. Add enough of the remaining flour to make a dough that is easy to handle. Turn onto a lightly floured surface. Knead for 10 minutes or until smooth and elastic. Place in a greased bowl, turning to coat the surface. Cover and let rise in a warm place for 1 hour or until doubled in bulk. Punch the dough down. Divide the dough into 2 equal portions. Roll each portion into a 9×18-inch rectangle. Roll up beginning at the short side and pressing the ends to seal and folding the ends under the loaves. Place seam side down in 2 greased and floured 5×9-inch loaf pans. Brush lightly with butter. Let rise for 1 hour or until doubled in bulk.

Place the pans on the lowest oven rack so that the tops of the pans are in the center of the oven. Do not allow the pans to touch. Bake at 425 degrees for 30 to 35 minutes or until golden brown and the loaves sound hollow when tapped. Remove the loaves to wire racks. Brush with butter. Let stand until cool.

Yield: 2 loaves

Three-Flour Bread

2 envelopes dry yeast
1 cup sifted all-purpose flour
1^1/2 cups whole wheat flour
^{1}/2 cup rye flour
2 cups milk

^{1}/2 cup packed brown sugar
3 tablespoons shortening
2 tablespoons sugar
1 tablespoon salt
2^1/4 to 2^1/2 cups sifted all-purpose flour

Mix the yeast, 1 cup all-purpose flour, whole wheat flour and rye flour in a large mixing bowl. Combine the milk, brown sugar, shortening, sugar and salt in a saucepan. Heat until warm, stirring constantly. Add to the flour mixture. Beat at low speed for 30 seconds, scraping the bowl constantly. Beat at high speed for 3 minutes. Add enough of the 2^1/4 to 2^1/2 cups all-purpose flour to make a moderately stiff dough, beating constantly. Turn onto a floured surface. Knead for 8 to 10 minutes or until smooth and elastic. Place in a greased bowl, turning to coat the surface. Cover and let rise for 1^1/2 hours or until doubled in bulk. Punch the dough down. Let rest for 10 minutes. Divide the dough into 2 equal portions. Shape each portion into a loaf. Place in 2 greased 5×9-inch loaf pans. Let rise for 45 to 60 minutes. Bake at 375 degrees for 40 minutes or until the loaves test done. Remove to wire racks to cool.

Yield: 2 loaves

SURVEYING THE WHEAT HARVEST AT
"HILL TOP" FARM OF A. B. HUEY, POCOPSON
TOWNSHIP, ON JULY 10, 1940.

Michigan Beer Cake

THIS VEGETABLE BREAD IS SERVED AS AN APPETIZER WITH BEER IN THE MIDWEST.

1¹/₂ cups chopped onions
1 large red bell pepper, chopped
1 green bell pepper, chopped
8 ounces mushrooms, chopped
¹/₂ cup chopped zucchini
3 tablespoons butter
12 large eggs

2¹/₂ cups flour
1 tablespoon Dijon mustard
Freshly ground pepper to taste
8 ounces Monterey Jack or Muenster
   cheese, shredded
6 ounces Cheddar cheese, shredded
2 tablespoons minced parsley

Sauté the onions, bell peppers, mushrooms and zucchini in the butter in a skillet for
5 minutes or just until cooked through. Remove the sautéed vegetables with a slotted spoon
to a platter lined with paper towels to drain. Beat the eggs in a mixing bowl for 2 to 3
minutes or until pale yellow. Add the flour. Beat for 1 minute longer or until thoroughly
combined. Add the Dijon mustard and pepper and beat well. Combine the drained
vegetable mixture, Monterey Jack cheese and Cheddar cheese in a large mixing bowl and
toss to mix well. Stir in the flour mixture. Add the parsley and mix well. Spoon into a
buttered 2-piece 10-inch tube pan. Tap the bottom of the pan against a hard surface to
remove any air bubbles. Bake at 325 degrees for 1¹/₂ hours or until the bread tests done.
Cool in the pan. Remove the bread from the pan and wrap in foil. Store in the refrigerator
for up to several days. Cut into thin slices to serve.

   Yield: 24 servings

Pepperoni Bread

1 loaf frozen bread dough
4 ounces provolone cheese, sliced
4 ounces mozzarella cheese, sliced

4 ounces pepperoni, sliced
4 ounces salami, sliced

Thaw the bread dough. Roll into an 11×14-inch rectangle. Place on a greased baking sheet.
Layer the provolone cheese, mozzarella cheese, pepperoni and salami down the center of
the rectangle. Fold each side over the center to enclose the filling, pinching the edges to
seal. Bake at 375 degrees for 30 minutes.

   Yield: 16 servings

Roquefort Popovers

1 1/2 cups milk
6 ounces Roquefort cheese, crumbled
1 teaspoon salt

Freshly ground pepper to taste
2 cups flour
6 large eggs

Grease popover or muffin cups generously with vegetable oil or shortening. Heat the milk and cheese in a saucepan over medium heat until the cheese is melted, stirring constantly. Remove from the heat. Whisk in the salt and pepper. Place the flour in a medium bowl. Add the cheese mixture and whisk just until combined. The batter may be lumpy. Add the eggs 1 at a time, whisking well after each addition. Pour into the prepared popover cups. Place on the lowest oven rack. Bake at 400 degrees for 20 minutes. Reduce the oven temperature to 350 degrees. Bake for 15 minutes longer or until fully puffed. Remove from the popover cups immediately to prevent sogginess. Poke the popovers with a knife to release the steam. Serve immediately.

Yield: 1 dozen popovers

Crumb Cake

1 cup sugar
2 tablespoons cinnamon
3 tablespoons ground nuts
3 tablespoons shredded coconut
3 cups flour
2 teaspoons baking soda

1 cup (2 sticks) butter, softened
2 cups sugar
2 teaspoons vanilla extract
1/2 teaspoon salt
4 eggs
2 cups sour cream

Mix 1 cup sugar, cinnamon, nuts and coconut in a bowl. Sift the flour and baking soda together. Beat the butter in a mixing bowl until creamy. Add 2 cups sugar and vanilla gradually, beating constantly until light and fluffy. Add the salt and eggs. Beat at high speed until blended. Add the flour mixture alternately with the sour cream, beating constantly. Pour 1/2 of the batter into a 9×13-inch cake pan. Sprinkle with 1/2 of the coconut mixture. Cut through the layers with a knife to marbleize. Pour the remaining batter over the layers. Sprinkle with the remaining coconut mixture. Cut through the layers again with a knife to marbleize. Bake at 350 degrees for 50 minutes or until the cake tests done.

Yield: 15 servings

Apple Cranberry Bread Pudding

KAREN L. MARTYNICK, COMMISSIONER

3/4 cup sugar
1 loaf Italian or French bread, thinly sliced
5 apples, peeled, cored, sliced
1 cup dried cranberries
6 eggs
4 cups milk or light cream
1 teaspoon vanilla extract

Reserve a small amount of the sugar. Alternate layers of the bread, apples, cranberries and remaining sugar in a buttered 9×13-inch baking pan, ending with the bread and a sprinkling of the reserved sugar. Beat the eggs, milk and vanilla in a mixing bowl until blended. Pour over the layers. Bake at 350 degrees for 1 hour. Serve warm with vanilla ice cream or custard sauce.

Yield: 15 servings

Apple Crumb Cake

1 (2-layer) package yellow cake mix
3 eggs
1 (15-ounce) can apple pie filling
3/4 cup flour
3/4 cup sugar
1/4 cup (1/2 stick) butter, softened

Combine the cake mix, eggs and apple pie filling in a mixing bowl and mix well. Spread in a greased 9×13-inch cake pan. Combine the flour, sugar and butter in a bowl and mix until crumbly. Sprinkle over the apple mixture. Bake at 350 degrees for 35 to 40 minutes or until the cake tests done.

Yield: 15 servings

Apple Custard Pye

Grate 4 sweet apples
for each pye; a pint
and a half of milk;
2 eggs; sugar, salt and
nutmeg and lemon
to taste. Bake as a
custard pye in a
quick oven.

Measure Cake

2 eggs; 1 cup of
sugar; 1/2 a cup of
butter; 1/2 a cup of
cream; 2 1/2 cups
flour; 1/2 a nutmeg
and 1/2 a teaspoonful
of saleratus (baking
soda). Let it be well
beat and add the
saleratus last. Bake
nearly an hour.

Cappuccino Biscotti

2 cups unbleached flour
1 cup sugar
1/2 teaspoon baking soda
1/2 teaspoon baking powder
1/2 teaspoon salt
1/2 teaspoon cinnamon
1/2 teaspoon ground cloves
5 tablespoons strong brewed espresso, cooled
4 teaspoons milk
1 large egg yolk
1 teaspoon vanilla extract
3/4 cup hazelnuts, toasted, skinned, coarsely chopped
1/2 cup semisweet chocolate chips

Mix the flour, sugar, baking soda, baking powder, salt, cinnamon
and cloves in a mixing bowl fitted with the paddle attachment.
Beat the espresso, milk, egg yolk and vanilla in a small bowl with
a wire whisk until blended. Add to the flour mixture and beat to
form a soft dough. Stir in the hazelnuts and chocolate chips.

Knead the dough several times on a lightly floured surface. Divide
the dough into 2 equal portions. Shape each portion into a 12-inch
log 2 inches wide. Place the logs 3 inches apart on a buttered large
baking sheet. Bake at 350 degrees for 35 minutes. Cool on the
baking sheet on a wire rack for 10 minutes. Reduce the oven
temperature to 300 degrees. Cut the logs diagonally into slices
3/4 inch thick. Arrange cut side down on the baking sheet. Bake
for 5 to 6 minutes on each side or until pale golden brown.
Remove to wire racks to cool. Store in airtight containers.

Yield: 32 biscotti

Cranberry Pistachio Biscotti

1¹/3 cups dried cranberries
2¹/2 cups unbleached flour
1 cup sugar
¹/2 teaspoon baking soda
¹/2 teaspoon baking powder
¹/2 teaspoon salt
3 large eggs
1 teaspoon vanilla extract
1 cup shelled natural pistachios
1 large egg
1 teaspoon water

Soak the cranberries in enough hot water to cover in a bowl for 5 minutes; drain. Pat dry with paper towels. Mix the flour, sugar, baking soda, baking powder and salt in a mixing bowl. Add 3 eggs and vanilla and beat to form a soft dough. Stir in the cranberries and pistachios.

Knead several times on a lightly floured surface. Divide the dough into 2 equal portions. Shape each portion into a 13-inch log 2 inches wide. Place the logs 3 inches apart on a buttered large baking sheet. Brush with a mixture of 1 egg and 1 teaspoon water. Bake at 325 degrees for 30 minutes. Cool on the baking sheet on a wire rack for 10 minutes. Cut the logs diagonally into slices ³/4 inch thick. Arrange cut side down on the baking sheet. Bake for 10 to 12 minutes on each side or until pale golden brown. Remove to wire racks to cool. Store in airtight containers.

Yield: 3 dozen biscotti

Ginger Chocolate Biscotti

2¹/₂ cups unbleached flour
1 cup sugar
1 teaspoon baking soda
¹/₂ teaspoon salt
¹/₄ teaspoon cinnamon
¹/₄ teaspoon cloves
2 tablespoons unsweetened Dutch-process baking cocoa
2 tablespoons grated peeled fresh gingerroot
¹/₂ teaspoon almond extract
3 large eggs
1¹/₄ cups blanched whole almonds, lightly toasted, coarsely chopped

Mix the flour, sugar, baking soda, salt, cinnamon, cloves and baking cocoa in a large mixing bowl. Combine the gingerroot, almond extract and eggs in a small bowl and beat well with a wire whisk. Add to the flour mixture and beat to form a soft dough. Stir in the almonds.

Knead the dough on a lightly floured surface several times. Divide the dough into 3 equal portions. Shape each portion into a 10-inch log 2¹/₂ inches wide. Place the logs 3 inches apart on a buttered and floured large baking sheet. Bake at 350 degrees for 25 minutes. Cool on the baking sheet on a wire rack for 10 minutes. Cut the logs diagonally into slices ³/₄ inch thick. Arrange cut side down on the baking sheet. Bake for 5 minutes on each side. Remove to wire racks to cool. Store in airtight containers.

Yield: 3 dozen biscotti

Meat AND Fish

SPONSORS: PENNSYLVANIA PORK PRODUCERS, SOUTHEAST CATTLEMEN'S ASSOCIATION

Santa Gertrudis cattle on the former King Ranch in western Chester County.

PENNSYLVANIA PORK PRODUCERS

The Pork Producers of Chester County take great pleasure in helping present to you the pork recipes in this chapter.

Today's pork isn't the meat that inspired phrases like "fat as a hog" and "eat like a pig." It has an average of 31 percent less fat, 14 percent fewer calories, and 10 percent less cholesterol than the pork your parents and grandparents ate when they were young.

The most important cooking tip for pork is don't overcook it. To ensure juicy, tender results, lean pork cuts should be cooked to medium doneness–160 degrees Fahrenheit. For small cuts–chops, kabobs, cutlets–cook until nicely browned, turning once. Use a meat thermometer to judge the doneness of roasts. When the internal temperature reaches 150 to 155 degrees Fahrenheit, remove the meat and let stand for 10 minutes. The meat's internal temperature will rise about 5 degrees after cooking.

SOUTHEAST CATTLEMEN'S ASSOCIATION

Chester County beef producers pride themselves in the top-quality products they produce for consumers. Then, properly cooked, beef can provide a quick ten-minute meal for those on the run or a lavish Sunday sit-down dinner. Beef provides essential nutrients and is an excellent source of protein and iron. Today, cattle is bred to produce very lean products while maintaining the taste and tenderness we have enjoyed for years. Beef cattle utilize ground that is unfit for grain production. Their main source of feed is grass, with a finishing ration of corn and soybeans. The Southeast Cattlemen's Association is pleased to help bring this selection of Chester County beef recipes to you.

ROLLED HAY IS SYNONYMOUS WITH CHESTER COUNTY'S RURAL COUNTRYSIDE.
CATTLE GRAZE IN THE LUSH FIELDS.

Taco Soup

1 pound ground beef
1 onion, chopped
1 garlic clove, chopped
1 to 2 (15-ounce) cans black beans, rinsed, drained
1 (10-ounce) can corn
1 (10-ounce) can diced tomatoes with jalapeño chiles
1 (4-ounce) can chopped green chiles
2 cups tomato juice
1 envelope ranch salad dressing mix
1 envelope taco seasoning mix

Brown the ground beef, onion and garlic in a skillet, stirring until the ground beef is crumbly; drain. Combine the ground beef mixture, black beans, undrained corn, tomatoes with jalapeño chiles, green chiles, tomato juice, ranch salad dressing mix and taco seasoning mix in a slow cooker and mix well. Cook on High for 8 hours or longer. The longer the soup cooks, the better the flavor. Serve with shredded Cheddar cheese, sour cream and crushed tortilla chips. You may use 1 cup spicy vegetable juice cocktail and 1 cup tomato sauce instead of the tomato juice.

Yield: 8 servings

Devault's Meatball Sauces

HISTORY OF DEVAULT FOODS

Devault Foods produces ever-popular "Philadelphia-Style" sandwich steaks, meatballs, hamburgers, ground beef, and their own Steakwich, plus a variety of specialty items. Through a national network of distributors, they serve customers ranging from emerging local chains to well-established national accounts as well as the restaurant/hotel industry and corporate, healthcare, educational, and military segments.

IN 1974 TOM FILLIPPO, PRESIDENT OF DEVAULT FOODS, ENVISIONED BEGINNING A NEW HOBBY OF MANUFACTURING MEATBALLS. TOM TESTED MANY MEATBALL RECIPES AND MET WITH NUMEROUS RESEARCH AND DEVELOPMENT TEAMS. HE THEN RECALLED HIS MOTHER HAD A FABULOUS MEATBALL RECIPE. THIS WAS THE RECIPE THAT WAS USED TO CREATE MRS. DIFILLIPPO'S MEATBALLS. DEMAND FOR HIS MOTHER'S MEATBALLS TURNED A HOBBY INTO DEVAULT'S MOST POPULAR PRODUCT.

Swedish Meatballs

> 2 cups beef bouillon
> 2 cups sour cream
> 1 teaspoon Worcestershire sauce
> $1/2$ cup chopped onion
> 2 to $2^1/2$ pounds Mrs. DiFillippo's Meatballs

Combine the bouillon, sour cream, Worcestershire sauce and onion in a skillet and blend well. Add the meatballs. Simmer for 45 minutes or until the meatballs are cooked through.

Yield: 4 servings

Since 1949
A Family Tradition of Excellence

Sweet-and-Sour Meatballs

1 (16-ounce) jar grape jelly
1 (16-ounce) jar chili sauce
2 to 2¹/₂ pounds Mrs. DiFillippo's Meatballs

Blend the jelly and chili sauce in a skillet. Add the meatballs.
Simmer for 45 minutes or until the meatballs are cooked through.
You may use one 20-ounce jar grape jelly, one 12-ounce jar chili
sauce and add 2 tablespoons brown sugar if desired.

Yield: 4 servings

"Souper" Meatballs

2 (10-ounce) cans cream of mushroom soup
2 cups sour cream
4 garlic cloves, minced
2 to 2¹/₂ pounds Mrs. DiFillippo's Meatballs

Blend the soup, sour cream and garlic in a skillet. Add the
meatballs. Simmer for 45 minutes or until the meatballs are
cooked through.

Yield: 4 servings

(HISTORY OF DEVAULT
FOODS *continued*)

Devault Foods
achieved tremendous
success supplying
patties to Wendy's
and Burger King.
Contact Information:
Devault Foods
1 Devault Lane
Devault, Pennsylvania
 19432
Phone:
 1-800-HAMBURG
Fax: 610-644-2527

Steak with Bleu Cheese Sauce

4 ounces Roquefort or other bleu cheese
4 teaspoons white wine
1 teaspoon lemon juice
1 tablespoon parsley, minced
1 garlic clove, crushed
$1/8$ teaspoon paprika
$1/8$ teaspoon pepper
1 tablespoon butter
4 rib or club steaks, cut 1 inch thick
Salt to taste

Mix the cheese, wine, lemon juice, parsley, garlic, paprika and pepper in a double boiler. Cook until smooth, stirring occasionally. Keep warm.

Heat the butter in a skillet until it begins to brown. Add the steaks. Cook until done to taste. Remove to a warm platter. Heat the pan drippings with a small amount of water or broth, stirring to deglaze the skillet. Season with salt. Add 2 tablespoons of the mixture to the cheese sauce. Pour over the steaks and serve immediately.

Yield: 4 servings

London Broil with Easy Bordelaise Sauce

1¹/₂ pounds flank steak
2 tablespoons ketchup
1 tablespoon soy sauce
1 garlic clove, minced
¹/₂ teaspoon thyme
¹/₄ teaspoon pepper
Easy Bordelaise Sauce

Score the steak diagonally across the grain on each side. Mix the ketchup, soy sauce, garlic, thyme and pepper in a small bowl. Brush over both sides of the steak. Let stand at room temperature for 30 to 45 minutes. Place on a rack in a broiler pan. Broil 4 inches from the heat source for 4 minutes. Turn the steak. Broil for 4 minutes or until the steak is medium-rare. Cut diagonally across the grain into slices ¹/₄ inch thick. Serve with Easy Bordelaise Sauce.

Yield: 2 or 3 servings

Easy Bordelaise Sauce

8 ounces mushrooms, sliced
¹/₄ cup (¹/₂ stick) butter
2 tablespoons flour
1 (10-ounce) can beef broth
1 tablespoon finely chopped parsley
¹/₄ teaspoon freshly ground pepper
¹/₈ teaspoon thyme
2 tablespoons dry red wine

Sauté the mushrooms in the butter in a skillet until the mushrooms begin to lose their juices. Sprinkle with the flour. Cook until the liquid is absorbed, stirring constantly. Stir in the beef broth gradually. Cook until the mixture comes to a boil and is thickened, stirring constantly. Stir in the parsley, pepper and thyme. Remove from the heat. Stir in the wine.

Yield: 2¹/₂ cups sauce

Beef Stir-Fry

EASY STEPS FOR
STIR-FRYING

* Freeze the beef
partially for easier
slicing. Cut the steak
into thin, uniform strips
or pieces. Marinate to
add flavor or tenderize
the beef while preparing
the other ingredients.
* Heat a small
amount of vegetable
oil in a wok or large
heavy skillet over
medium-high heat.
*Stir-fry the beef in
8-ounce batches until
the beef is no longer
pink, adding additional
vegetable oil as needed.
*Stir-fry the beef and
vegetables separately
and then combine
and heat through.
Thicken the liquid with
cornstarch dissolved in
water if desired.

1 pound beef top round or boneless sirloin steak,
    cut $3/4$ inch thick
$1/4$ cup soy sauce
1 tablespoon cornstarch
1 tablespoon dark sesame oil
2 teaspoons minced fresh gingerroot, or $1/2$ teaspoon ginger
$1/2$ cup water
12 ounces green beans, cut into 2-inch pieces
3 cups water
2 (3-ounce) packages instant ramen noodles
1 tablespoon vegetable oil
1 (8-ounce) can sliced water chestnuts, drained
$1/2$ cup beef broth

Trim the steak. Cut the steak into halves lengthwise. Cut each
half into strips $1/8$ inch thick. Combine the soy sauce, cornstarch,
sesame oil and gingerroot in a bowl and mix well. Add the beef,
stirring to coat.

Bring $1/2$ cup water to a boil in a large skillet or wok over medium-
high heat. Add the green beans. Cook, covered, for 8 to 10 minutes
or until tender. Remove the green beans with a slotted spoon to a
platter and keep warm. Add 3 cups water to the skillet. Bring to a
boil. Crumble the ramen noodles, reserving the seasoning packets
for another purpose. Add the ramen noodles to the boiling water.
Cook for 3 minutes. Drain and rinse the noodles. Place on a platter
and keep warm.

Drain the beef, reserving the marinade. Heat the vegetable oil
in the skillet. Add $1/2$ of the beef. Stir-fry for 1 to 2 minutes or
until the surface is no longer pink. Do not overcook. Remove from
the skillet with a slotted spoon and keep warm. Repeat with the
remaining beef. Return the beef and green beans to the skillet.
Add the water chestnuts, broth and reserved marinade. Cook until
the sauce is thickened and bubbly, stirring constantly. Add the
ramen noodles and toss to mix.

Yield: 4 servings

Two-Way Shredded Beef

1 medium onion, cut into quarters
3 garlic cloves, peeled
1 (3- to 3^1/$_4$-pound) boneless beef chuck shoulder or
    bottom round roast, cut into 4 large pieces
1 teaspoon salt
^{1}/$_2$ teaspoon pepper
^{3}/$_4$ cup water

Place the onion and garlic in a slow cooker. Arrange the beef over the vegetables. Sprinkle with the salt and pepper. Add the water. Cook, covered, on Low for 9 to 9^1/$_2$ hours or until the beef is tender. Remove the beef from the cooking liquid and cool slightly. Trim and discard any excess fat from the beef. Shred the beef using 2 forks. Strain the cooking liquid, discarding the solids and skimming off the fat. Reserve ^{1}/$_2$ cup of the liquid. Pour over the shredded beef. Use to make sandwiches. You may store, covered, in the refrigerator for up to 4 days or freeze and thaw before using. The beef may also be shredded in a food processor.

Yield: 7^1/$_2$ cups shredded beef

Tex-Mex Beef Wraps with Tomato Corn Salsa

1/2 cup frozen whole kernel corn, thawed
1 small tomato, chopped
1 (16-ounce) jar thick and chunky salsa
1 tablespoon chopped cilantro
3 3/4 cups Two-Way Shredded Beef (page 121)
2 tablespoons chopped cilantro
4 (10-inch) flour tortillas, warmed
Chopped cilantro to taste

Combine the corn, tomato, 2 tablespoons of the salsa and 1 tablespoon cilantro in a bowl and mix well. Chill, covered, in the refrigerator.

Combine the Two-Way Shredded Beef, remaining salsa and 2 tablespoons cilantro in a 1 1/2-quart microwave-safe dish. Microwave, covered, on High for 7 to 8 minutes or until heated through, stirring once. Spoon the beef mixture evenly over each tortilla, leaving 1 1/2-inch border around the edge. Top each with the corn mixture. Fold the right and left edges of the tortillas over the filling. Fold the bottom edges up and roll up. Sprinkle with cilantro to taste.

Yield: 4 servings

Honey Mustard Barbecue Beefwiches

3³/4 cups Two-Way Shredded Beef (page 121)
1 cup honey mustard barbecue sauce or favorite barbecue sauce
4 hamburger buns or Kaiser rolls, split
Chopped green bell pepper to taste
Chopped sweet onion to taste

Combine the Two-Way Shredded Beef and barbecue sauce in a 1¹/2-quart microwave-safe dish and mix well. Microwave, covered, on High for 5 to 6 minutes or until heated through, stirring once. Place the beef mixture on the bottom half of each bun. Layer bell pepper and onion over the beef. Replace the top half of the bun.

Yield: 4 servings

Mediterranean Beef Pot Roast and Vegetables

8 (2- to 2^1/2-inch-thick) new potatoes
8 ounces peeled baby carrots
4 garlic cloves, peeled
1 (3- to 3^1/4-pound) boneless beef bottom round rump roast or chuck shoulder roast
1 teaspoon crushed rosemary
1 teaspoon salt
^{1}/2 teaspoon pepper
^{1}/4 cup water
^{1}/4 cup dry red wine
2 tablespoons cornstarch
2 tablespoons water
Chopped fresh parsley

Place the potatoes, carrots and garlic in a slow cooker. Rub the roast with the rosemary, salt and pepper. Place on top of the vegetables. Add ^{1}/4 cup water and wine. Cook, covered, on Low for 10 to 11 hours or until the beef and vegetables are tender. Remove the roast from the slow cooker and trim. Arrange the roast and vegetables on a serving platter and keep warm.

Strain the cooking liquid, skimming the fat and discarding the solids. Reserve 2 cups of the cooking liquid. Mix the cornstarch and 2 tablespoons water in a bowl. Combine the reserved liquid and cornstarch mixture in a small saucepan and blend well. Bring to a boil. Cook for 1 minute or until thickened, stirring constantly.

To serve, cut the roast across the grain into thin slices. Sprinkle with parsley. Serve with the gravy.

Yield: 6 to 8 servings

Stuffed Green Bell Peppers

5 green bell peppers
1 pound ground beef
1 teaspoon salt
$^1/_4$ teaspoon pepper
1 medium onion, chopped
1 (8-ounce) can tomatoes, crushed
4 cups salted cooked rice
2 teaspoons Worcestershire sauce
1 tablespoon minced parsley
1 cup shredded Cheddar cheese

Cut off the tops of the bell peppers and reserve. Remove the seeds. Place the bell peppers in a 2$^1/_2$-quart baking dish. Brown the ground beef in a skillet, stirring until crumbly. Season with the salt and pepper. Add the onion. Cook until the onion is tender; drain. Add the undrained crushed tomatoes, cooked rice, Worcestershire sauce and parsley. Simmer for 5 minutes. Stir in the cheese. Stuff into the bell peppers, packing the extra rice mixture around the bell peppers. Top the stuffed bell peppers with the reserved tops. Bake, covered, at 350 degrees for 40 to 45 minutes or until cooked through. Let stand for 15 minutes before serving. You may use 2 fresh tomatoes, chopped, instead of the canned tomatoes.

Yield: 5 servings

(SLOW-COOKER TIPS continued)

*Chilled ingredients may be placed directly in a slow cooker.
*Thaw vegetables slightly before placing in a slow cooker. When using frozen meat, add about 1 cup warm liquid to the slow cooker first to help prevent sudden temperature changes.
*Vegetables tend to cook slower than meat in a slow cooker. Place vegetables on the bottom and around the side and meat on top.
*Trim any visible fat from the meat prior to placing in a slow cooker.
*Since liquid from food cooked in a slow cooker accumulates, only small amounts of liquid need to be added.

Savory Summer Hamburgers

4 pounds ground beef or ground venison, or a mixture of both
1/4 cup Worcestershire sauce
1/4 cup soy sauce
1 teaspoon salt
1 teaspoon pepper
2 eggs, beaten
1 large onion, finely chopped
1/2 cup bread crumbs
1/2 cup milk
1 cup shredded Cheddar cheese

Combine the ground beef, Worcestershire sauce, soy sauce, salt and pepper in a bowl and mix well. Add the eggs, onion, bread crumbs and milk and mix well. Add the cheese and mix well. Shape into patties. Wrap each patty in waxed paper and place in a large sealable plastic freezer bag. Store in the freezer until ready to use.

Yield: 8 patties

THE "HIGHPOINT-ACRES" FARMHOUSE
WAS BUILT WITH LOCAL FIELDSTONE.

Reuben Pie

8 ounces ground chuck
1 egg, beaten
1/3 cup evaporated milk
3/4 cup soft rye bread crumbs (about
 1 slice rye bread)
1/4 cup chopped onion
1/2 teaspoon prepared mustard

1/4 teaspoon salt
1/8 teaspoon pepper
1 (8-ounce) can sauerkraut, drained,
 chopped
1 (12-ounce) can corned beef, flaked
1 (10-inch) deep-dish pie shell
4 ounces Swiss cheese, grated

Brown the ground chuck in a skillet, stirring until crumbly; drain. Combine the egg, evaporated milk, bread crumbs, onion, mustard, salt and pepper in a bowl and mix well. Add the ground chuck, sauerkraut and corned beef and mix well. Spread 1/2 of the sauerkraut mixture in the pie shell. Sprinkle with 1/2 of the cheese. Cover with the remaining sauerkraut mixture. Top with the remaining cheese. Place the pie on a baking sheet. Bake at 400 degrees for 30 minutes or until cooked through and the crust is brown. Serve with tossed salad and applesauce.

Yield: 4 servings

Shepherd's Pie

BOB FLICK, STATE REPRESENTATIVE

1 pound ground beef
1 medium onion, chopped
1 medium green bell pepper, chopped
1 (16-ounce) can whole kernel corn,
 drained

1 (10-ounce) can tomato soup
2 cups mashed cooked potatoes
Paprika to taste
Shredded Cheddar cheese to taste

Brown the ground beef with the onion and bell pepper in a skillet, stirring until the ground beef is crumbly; drain. Stir in the corn and tomato soup. Simmer for 5 minutes. Spread in an 8×8-inch baking dish. Spread the mashed potatoes over the ground beef mixture. Sprinkle with paprika and cheese. Bake at 350 degrees for 30 minutes or until the top is light brown. You may substitute your favorite cheese for the Cheddar cheese.

Yield: 4 servings

Veal Scaloppine

1 pound veal cutlet, thinly sliced
1/2 cup flour
6 tablespoons butter
Salt and pepper to taste
1/4 cup sherry or marsala
2 tablespoons chopped fresh parsley
1 (4-ounce) can sliced mushrooms, drained
Chopped fresh parsley to taste

Pound the veal flat using a meat mallet. Coat the veal with the flour. Sauté the veal in the butter in a large skillet for 3 to 4 minutes on each side. Sprinkle with salt and pepper. Add the wine, 2 tablespoons parsley and mushrooms. Simmer for 10 minutes. Sprinkle with parsley to taste.

Yield: 4 servings

Venetian-Style Calves' Livers

1 pound calves' livers
4 medium onions, thinly sliced
1/4 cup (1/2 stick) butter
1/4 cup dry white wine
2 tablespoons finely chopped fresh parsley

Cut the livers into thin strips about 2 inches long. Sauté the onions in the butter in a large skillet over low heat for 15 minutes. Add the livers. Cook over medium heat for 3 to 4 minutes or until the livers are light brown. Add the wine, stirring to deglaze the skillet. Sprinkle with the parsley just before serving.

Yield: 4 servings

Lamb Gyros with Cucumber Yogurt Sauce

1 pound lean ground lamb
2 garlic cloves, crushed
1$\frac{1}{2}$ teaspoons crushed oregano
1 teaspoon onion powder
1 teaspoon salt
$\frac{3}{4}$ teaspoon pepper
4 whole pita bread rounds, cut into halves, warmed
1 large tomato, cut into halves, sliced
1 small onion, thinly sliced
Cucumber Yogurt Sauce

Combine the lamb, garlic, oregano, onion powder, salt and pepper in a large bowl and mix gently. Shape into 2 oval patties $\frac{1}{2}$ inch thick. Place on a rack in a broiler pan. Broil 3 to 4 inches from the heat source for 8 to 10 minutes or until cooked through, turning once. Cut each patty into thin slices. Fill each pita bread half with the lamb patty slices, tomato and onion. Serve with Cucumber Yogurt Sauce.

Yield: 4 servings

Cucumber Yogurt Sauce

1 cup plain reduced-fat yogurt
$\frac{1}{3}$ cup chopped seeded cucumber
2 tablespoons finely chopped onion
1 garlic clove, crushed
1 teaspoon sugar

Combine the yogurt, cucumber, onion, garlic and sugar in a medium bowl and mix well. Chill, covered, in the refrigerator.

Yield: 1$\frac{1}{3}$ cups sauce

Lamb Kabobs

1/4 cup olive oil
1/4 cup lemon juice
1 garlic clove, crushed
1 teaspoon ginger
1 teaspoon coriander
1/2 teaspoon curry powder
1 teaspoon garlic salt
1 teaspoon salt
1 pound lamb shoulder or leg, cut into 2-inch squares
8 fresh whole mushrooms
8 cherry tomatoes
1 green bell pepper, cut into strips

Mix the olive oil, lemon juice, garlic, ginger, coriander, curry powder, garlic salt and salt in a bowl and mix well. Add the lamb and toss to coat. Marinate, covered, in the refrigerator for 2 to 3 hours, turning occasionally. Drain the lamb, reserving the marinade. Boil the reserved marinade in a saucepan for 2 to 3 minutes, stirring frequently. Arrange the lamb, mushrooms, cherry tomatoes and bell pepper alternately on skewers. Place on a grill rack or on a rack in a broiler pan. Grill or broil until the lamb is cooked to the desired degree of doneness, turning and basting frequently with the cooked marinade.

Yield: 4 servings

Peppered Pork Roast

1 (2- to 4-pound) boneless pork roast
1 to 2 teaspoons garlic pepper
1 to 2 teaspoons crushed rosemary

Coat the pork with a mixture of the garlic pepper and rosemary. Place in a shallow baking pan. Bake at 350 degrees for 45 to 90 minutes or until a meat thermometer inserted in the thickest portion registers 160 degrees. Remove from the oven. Let stand for 5 to 10 minutes before slicing to serve.

Yield: 6 servings

Cranberry-Glazed Pork Roast

2 teaspoons cornstarch
$^1/_2$ teaspoon grated orange zest
$^1/_4$ teaspoon cinnamon
$^1/_8$ teaspoon salt
2 tablespoons orange juice
2 tablespoons dry sherry
1 (16-ounce) can whole cranberry sauce
1 (4-pound) boneless pork loin roast
1 large red onion, cut into 6 to 8 wedges, or 12 small onions

Mix the cornstarch, orange zest, cinnamon and salt in a small saucepan. Stir in the orange juice, sherry and cranberry sauce. Cook over medium heat until thickened, stirring constantly. Place the pork in a shallow roasting pan. Roast at 325 degrees for 1 hour. Place the onion wedges around the pork. Spoon $^1/_2$ cup of the cranberry mixture over the pork and onion. Roast for 30 to 60 minutes or until a meat thermometer inserted in the thickest portion registers 160 degrees. Let stand for 5 to 10 minutes before slicing. Serve with the remaining cranberry mixture.

Yield: 16 servings

THE SILO, AN INTEGRAL COMPONENT OF
CHESTER COUNTY FARMING, STANDS MAJESTIC AT
"HIGHPOINT-ACRES" IN NEW GARDEN TOWNSHIP.

Roast Pork with Spiced Cherry Sauce

1 (3- to 4-pound) boneless pork loin roast
1 teaspoon sage
1 teaspoon salt
1 teaspoon pepper
1 (16-ounce) can tart red pitted cherries
1^1/$_2$ cups sugar
^{1}/$_4$ cup vinegar
12 whole cloves
1 (3-inch) cinnamon stick
^{1}/$_3$ cup cornstarch
1 tablespoon lemon juice
1 tablespoon butter or margarine
3 or 4 drops of red food coloring (optional)

Rub the pork with the sage, salt and pepper. Place in an ungreased shallow baking pan. Bake, uncovered, at 325 degrees for 1^1/$_2$ to 2 hours or until a meat thermometer inserted in the thickest portion registers 160 to 170 degrees. Remove from the oven. Let stand for 10 minutes before slicing.

Drain the cherries, reserving the liquid. Add enough water to the reserved liquid to measure ^{3}/$_4$ cup. Pour ^{1}/$_2$ cup of the cherry mixture into a saucepan. Add the sugar, vinegar, cloves and cinnamon. Bring to a boil and reduce the heat. Simmer, uncovered, for 10 minutes. Remove the cloves and cinnamon stick. Mix the cornstarch and remaining cherry mixture in a small bowl until smooth. Add to the saucepan. Bring to a boil. Cook for 2 minutes, stirring constantly. Stir in the lemon juice, butter, cherries and food coloring. Cook until heated through. Serve with the sliced pork.

Yield: 8 to 10 servings

Maple Mustard-Glazed Pork Roast

2/3 cup maple syrup
3 tablespoons Dijon mustard
2 tablespoons cider vinegar
2 tablespoons soy sauce
Salt and pepper to taste
1 (2-pound) boneless pork loin roast

Combine the maple syrup, Dijon mustard, vinegar, soy sauce and salt and pepper in a bowl and mix well. Spread evenly over the pork. Place in a shallow roasting pan. Bake at 350 degrees for 45 to 75 minutes or until a meat thermometer inserted into the thickest portion registers 160 degrees. Remove the pork from the oven. Let rest for 10 minutes before slicing to serve.

Yield: 6 servings

Barbecued Pork Tenderloin

1 cup soy sauce
1/3 cup toasted dark sesame oil
3 garlic cloves, minced
1 tablespoon ginger
1 (2- to 3-pound) pork tenderloin
1 (16-ounce) bottle Old Masterpiece barbecue sauce
1/3 cup dark sesame oil
1/3 cup soy sauce
1 large garlic clove, minced

Mix 1 cup soy sauce, 1/3 cup sesame oil, 3 garlic cloves and ginger in a sealable plastic food storage bag. Add the pork, turning to coat. Seal the bag. Marinate in the refrigerator for 6 to 12 hours. Drain the pork, discarding the marinade. Place on a grill rack. Grill off the flame at 200 degrees for 3 to 4 hours or until a meat thermometer inserted into the thickest portion registers 180 degrees. Let rest for 10 minutes. Heat the barbecue sauce, 1/3 cup sesame oil, 1/3 cup soy sauce and 1 garlic clove in a saucepan, stirring to mix well. Cut the pork into slices and baste with the warm sauce.

Yield: 4 to 6 servings

Maple-Glazed Pork Tenderloins

2^1/$_2$ teaspoons salt
^{1}/$_4$ teaspoon pepper
2 (12-ounce) pork tenderloins
6 slices bacon
^{1}/$_2$ (24-ounce) bottle maple syrup

Rub the salt and pepper into the tenderloins. Place in a medium bowl. Chill, covered, for 4 hours or longer. Arrange the tenderloins with the thick ends pointing away from each other and the thin ends slightly overlapping to make a piece of pork of even thickness. Wrap with the bacon slices and secure with small metal skewers. Place on a grill rack.

Grill over medium heat for 25 to 30 minutes or until a meat thermometer inserted into the thickest portion registers 170 degrees, brushing frequently with maple syrup and turning the pork occasionally. Remove the skewers from the pork. You may place the pork on a rack in a broiler pan and bake 7 to 9 inches from the heat source at 450 degrees for 30 to 40 minutes or until the pork tests done, brushing frequently with the maple syrup.

Yield: 6 servings

Southern Skillet Barbecued Pork

1/4 cup reduced-calorie Italian salad dressing
1/4 cup barbecue sauce
1 teaspoon chili powder
4 boneless pork chops, 3/8 inch thick

Mix the salad dressing, barbecue sauce and chili powder in a bowl. Place the pork chops in a sealable plastic food storage bag. Add the marinade and seal the bag. Marinate in the refrigerator for 30 minutes to 12 hours. Drain the pork chops, reserving the marinade.

Heat a nonstick skillet over medium-high heat. Add the pork chops. Cook until brown on each side. Add the reserved marinade. Cover and simmer over medium heat for 4 to 5 minutes or until the pork chops test done.

Yield: 4 servings

FARM BUILDINGS AT "HIGHPOINT-ACRES" IN
NEW GARDEN TOWNSHIP.

Pork Chops with Caramelized Apples

4 pork loin chops, 1 1/2 inches thick
2 teaspoons crushed thyme leaves
1/2 teaspoon salt
1 1/2 teaspoons pepper
6 tablespoons butter
3/4 cup sugar
4 large tart apples, cored, peeled, cut into wedges
Vegetable oil

Season each side of the pork chops with the thyme, salt and pepper. Melt the butter and sugar in a large heavy skillet over medium-high heat. Add the apples. Sauté for 30 to 40 minutes or until the apples begin to brown. Turn the apples. Cook for 5 minutes or until the apples are golden brown and the sauce is thickened. Remove from the heat and keep warm.

Brown the pork chops in a small amount of vegetable oil in a heavy skillet over medium-high heat for 4 minutes on each side. Continue to cook the pork chops or until a meat thermometer inserted in the thickest portion registers 160 degrees, turning every 2 minutes. The total cooking time for the pork chops will be 12 to 15 minutes. Serve the pork chops with the apples.

Yield: 4 servings

Coriander Pepper Pork Chops

3 tablespoons soy sauce
1 tablespoon brown sugar
2 garlic cloves, crushed
1 tablespoon crushed coriander seeds
1 tablespoon coarsely ground pepper
4 boneless pork chops, about 1 inch thick

Mix the soy sauce, brown sugar, garlic, coriander seeds and pepper in a bowl. Place the pork chops in a shallow dish. Pour the marinade over the pork chops. Marinate for 30 minutes. Drain the pork chops, discarding the marinade. Place the pork chops on a grill rack. Grill over medium-hot coals for 7 to 8 minutes or until a meat thermometer inserted into the thickest portion registers 160 degrees, turning once.

Yield: 4 servings

City Pork Kabobs with Creamy Mushroom Sauce

4 boneless pork chops, cut into 1-inch cubes
3/4 cup finely crushed rich round crackers
1 tablespoon parsley flakes
1 teaspoon crushed basil
1 teaspoon paprika
1/2 teaspoon garlic salt
1/2 teaspoon poultry seasoning
1/4 teaspoon pepper
1 egg, beaten
1 (10-ounce) can cream of mushroom soup
1 (4-ounce) can mushroom stems and pieces, drained
1/2 cup milk
1 teaspoon crushed basil
1/2 cup sour cream
2 cups hot cooked noodles

Thread the pork onto eight 9-inch skewers. Mix the cracker crumbs, parsley, 1 teaspoon basil, paprika, garlic salt, poultry seasoning and pepper in a shallow dish. Brush the pork with the beaten egg and roll in the crumb mixture until lightly coated. Arrange in a shallow baking pan. Bake, uncovered, at 400 degrees for 15 to 18 minutes or until the pork is cooked through and golden brown.

Combine the soup, mushrooms, milk and 1 teaspoon basil in a small saucepan and mix well. Bring to a boil and reduce the heat, stirring constantly. Stir in the sour cream. Cook until heated through; do not boil.

To serve, arrange the kabobs over the noodles on individual serving plates. Spoon the sauce over the top.

Yield: 4 servings

Barbecued Babyback Ribs

4 pounds babyback ribs
1 onion, peeled, quartered
4 cloves
2 peppercorns
2 teaspoons salt
2 cups beer
$^1/_2$ cup honey
$^2/_3$ cup soy sauce
$^2/_3$ cup ketchup
1 teaspoon dry mustard
1 teaspoon paprika
1 teaspoon salt
1 cup red wine vinegar
1 cup orange juice
$^1/_2$ teaspoon hot pepper sauce
1 garlic clove, finely mashed

Cut the ribs into 4-rib sections or leave whole. Place the ribs, onion, cloves, peppercorns, 2 teaspoons salt and beer in a large stockpot. Bring to a boil and reduce the heat. Simmer for 10 to 15 minutes or until partially cooked through. Drain the ribs, discarding the stock.

Combine the honey, soy sauce, ketchup, dry mustard, paprika, 1 teaspoon salt, red wine vinegar, orange juice, hot pepper sauce and garlic in a saucepan and mix well. Bring to a boil and reduce the heat. Simmer for 10 minutes. Place the ribs in a sealable plastic bag. Add the marinade and seal the bag. Marinate in the refrigerator for 8 to 12 hours. Drain the ribs, reserving the marinade. Place the reserved marinade in a saucepan. Boil for 2 to 3 minutes. Place the ribs on a grill rack. Grill for 10 to 20 minutes or until cooked through, turning several times and brushing with the heated marinade. Watch closely to prevent burning.

Yield: 2 to 4 servings

Art Hershey's Barbecue Sauce

THIS BARBECUE SAUCE CAN BE SERVED AT A "PIG ROAST" OR MIXED WITH ROAST PORK FOR PORK BARBECUE SANDWICHES. "WHEN ROASTING A PIG WE PREPARE 5 GALLONS OF BREAD STUFFING FOR THE PIG. THE 200-POUND PIG IS STUFFED AND PUT INTO A CHARCOAL-FIRED OVEN FOR 12 TO 14 HOURS."

—ART HERSHEY, STATE REPRESENTATIVE

2 beef bouillon cubes
2 cups boiling water
1 (10-ounce) bottle ketchup
1 (6-ounce) can tomato paste
1 cup wine vinegar
2 tablespoons mustard
1 tablespoon Worcestershire sauce
$1/2$ cup packed brown sugar
Onion salt to taste
Several drops of Tabasco sauce

Dissolve the bouillon cubes in the boiling water in a saucepan. Add the ketchup, tomato paste, wine vinegar, mustard, Worcestershire sauce, brown sugar, onion salt and Tabasco sauce and mix well. Bring to a boil and reduce the heat. Simmer until smooth.

Yield: $1^1/2$ quarts sauce

BULL BEING SHOWN AT THE WEST
CHESTER FAIR, 1914.

Dutch Goose

5 carrots, sliced
4 potatoes, cut into pieces
1 large onion, cut into pieces
2 large ribs celery, sliced
2 tablespoons butter
7 or 8 bread slices, torn
1 pound sausage
1 pint oysters and liquor
$1/2$ cup raisins
1 pig stomach
1 tablespoon butter
Saffron to taste

Parboil the carrots and potatoes in a small amount of water in a saucepan. Sauté the onion and celery in 2 tablespoons butter in a skillet. Add the bread. Brown the sausage in a skillet, stirring until crumbly; drain. Combine the carrots, potatoes, onion mixture, sausage, oysters and raisins in a large bowl and mix well. Stuff into the pig stomach. Rub with 1 tablespoon butter and saffron. Place in a baking pan. Place any leftover stuffing around the stomach. Bake at 350 degrees for 2 hours.

Yield: 4 servings

Saumon en Croûte (Salmon in Crust)

2 pounds salmon fillet
Salt and pepper to taste
2 medium onions or shallots, finely chopped
Clarified butter
3 packages fresh leaf spinach, blanched, chopped
1 (17-ounce) package puff pastry
1 egg
1/2 cup white wine
2 tablespoons water
2 cups heavy cream
2 tablespoons butter
2 tablespoons flour

Sear the fish in a skillet until light brown on each side. Season with salt and pepper. Remove from the heat and cool. Sauté the onions in clarified butter in a skillet over medium heat until transparent. Remove from the heat. Remove 1/2 of the onions to a platter and reserve for the sauce. Add the spinach to the remaining onions in the skillet and mix well.

Roll the puff pastry on a lightly floured surface about 3/8 inch thick or until large enough to enclose the fish. Place the fish on half of the pastry. Cover with the spinach mixture. Brush the edges with a mixture of the egg and a small amount of water. Cover the fish with the remaining half of the puff pastry and seal the edges to enclose. Place in a baking dish. Bake at 375 degrees for 20 minutes.

Combine the wine, 2 tablespoons water and reserved onions in a saucepan. Bring to a boil. Cook until the liquid is reduced by 1/3. Add the cream. Return to a boil. Melt 2 tablespoons butter in a saucepan. Stir in the flour. Heat to form a roux, stirring constantly. Stir into the cream mixture a small amount at a time. Cook until thickened and smooth, stirring constantly. Season with salt and pepper to taste. Serve with the pastry.

Note: To clarify butter, melt the butter in a saucepan over low heat until foamy. Remove from the heat and let stand until the milk solids settle to the bottom of the saucepan and the salt crystals settle on the top. Skim the salt crystals and carefully pour the butter oil into a separate container. Discard the milk solids that have settled to the bottom.

Yield: 8 servings

Linguini with White Clam Sauce

2 (8-ounce) cans minced clams
1 large onion, chopped
1 garlic clove, minced
3 tablespoons chopped fresh parsley
1/3 cup olive oil
1/2 teaspoon salt
1/4 teaspoon pepper
1/4 cup dry white wine (optional)
1 pound linguini, cooked, drained
Sprigs of fresh parsley
Grated Parmesan cheese

Drain the clams, reserving the liquid. Sauté the onion, garlic and 3 tablespoons parsley in the olive oil in a saucepan until the onion is transparent. Season with the salt and pepper. Add the wine and reserved clam liquid. Simmer for 5 minutes. Add the clams. Cook until heated through. Do not boil or the clams will become tough. Arrange the pasta on a warm serving platter. Pour the clam sauce over the pasta. Garnish with sprigs of fresh parsley. Serve with Parmesan cheese.

Yield: 6 servings

1492 Crab Cakes

PAUL O'TOOLE, HARTEFELD NATIONAL GOLF COURSE AND RESTAURANT

1 small onion, minced
1/2 cup minced celery
1 teaspoon butter
1 cup mayonnaise
1 egg
1 teaspoon Old Bay seasoning
1/2 teaspoon dry mustard
1/4 teaspoon Worcestershire sauce
2 tablespoons chopped parsley
1/4 teaspoon cayenne pepper
1 drop of Tabasco sauce
Salt and black pepper to taste
1 pound jumbo lump crab meat
Flour
Clarified butter

Sauté the onion and celery in 1 teaspoon butter in a skillet until the onion is translucent. Remove from the heat to cool. Combine the mayonnaise, egg, Old Bay seasoning, mustard, Worcestershire sauce, parsley, cayenne pepper, Tabasco sauce and salt and black pepper in a bowl and mix well. Add the sautéed vegetables and crab meat and stir to mix well. Chill, covered, for 1 hour.

Shape the crab meat mixture into 4-ounce patties. Dredge in flour. Sauté in clarified butter in a skillet until golden brown on each side.

Note: To clarify butter, melt the butter in a saucepan over low heat until foamy. Remove from the heat and let stand until the milk solids settle to the bottom of the saucepan and the salt crystals settle on the top. Skim the salt crystals and carefully pour the butter oil into a separate container. Discard the milk solids that have settled to the bottom.

Yield: 4 to 6 servings

Shrimp with Feta Cheese

1 onion, chopped
1 garlic clove, crushed
3 tablespoons olive oil
8 large tomatoes, peeled, coarsely chopped
2 tablespoons tomato paste
1/2 cup dry white wine
1 teaspoon oregano
4 parsley sprigs, chopped
Salt and pepper to taste
6 ounces feta cheese, cut into 1-inch cubes
1 pound large shrimp, peeled, deveined
Hot cooked orzo

Sauté the onion and garlic in the olive oil in a skillet until transparent. Add the undrained tomatoes, tomato paste, wine and oregano. Simmer for 20 to 30 minutes or until some of the liquid is evaporated and the mixture is thickened. Add the parsley, salt and pepper. Stir in the cheese and shrimp. Cook for 2 to 3 minutes or until the shrimp turn pink. Do not overcook or the shrimp will become tough. Serve over orzo with chunks of peasant bread.

Yield: 4 servings

Shrimp Tarragon

1/2 cup (1 stick) butter, melted
2 tablespoons chopped fresh tarragon, or 1 tablespoon dried tarragon
2 pounds uncooked shrimp, peeled, deveined
1/2 cup heavy cream
1/8 teaspoon Tabasco sauce
1/4 teaspoon salt
Hot cooked rice

Melt the butter in a skillet. Stir in the tarragon. Add the shrimp. Cook until the shrimp turn pink. Add the cream and Tabasco sauce. Bring just to the boiling point. Do not boil. Sprinkle with the salt. Serve over rice.

Yield: 4 servings

Fusilli with Shrimp and Fresh Vegetable Sauce

4 quarts water
2 pounds shrimp, peeled, deveined
2 medium yellow bell peppers, cut into $^1/_4$-inch pieces
2 medium red bell peppers, cut into $^1/_4$-inch pieces
6 plum tomatoes, cut into $^1/_2$-inch pieces
$^1/_2$ cup chopped fresh dill
2 tablespoons chopped fresh tarragon, or 2 teaspoons dried tarragon
2 tablespoons chopped shallots
2 tablespoons hot red pepper flakes
1 teaspoon freshly ground black pepper
1 teaspoon salt
$^1/_2$ cup lemon juice
1 cup olive oil
$^1/_4$ teaspoon hot chili oil
4 quarts water
1 medium head broccoli, cut into florets
1$^1/_2$ cups cooked shelled peas
1 pound fusilli or linguini, cooked, drained

Bring 4 quarts water to a boil in a medium saucepan. Add the shrimp. Cook for 1 minute
or until the shrimp turn pink; drain. Rinse under cold running water to stop the cooking
process; drain. Place in a large serving bowl. Add the bell peppers, tomatoes, dill, tarragon,
shallots, red pepper flakes, black pepper, salt, lemon juice, olive oil and chili oil and toss to
mix well. Chill, covered, for 2 hours or longer.

Bring 4 quarts water to a boil in a medium saucepan. Add the broccoli. Cook for 1 minute;
drain. Rinse under cold running water to stop the cooking process; drain. Toss with the peas
in a bowl. Remove the shrimp mixture from the refrigerator and let stand for 15 minutes.
Add the broccoli mixture and toss to mix well. Add the hot cooked pasta and toss to mix
well. Serve immediately. You may purchase hot chili oil at an oriental grocery store.

Yield: 6 servings

Poultry

A gaggle of geese in a Chester County barn.

Chester County's poultry farms are located mainly along the western edge of the county. Most are very large operations, but some small egg-laying operations still exist. In 1999, Chester County produced two million broilers with a value of $3,848,000, ranking the county fourteenth in the state. Total value of egg production in the county was $4,869,000, ranking the county ninth in the state. The average number of layers on Chester County farms was 399,000. Hens lay an average of 271 eggs per year. There are two major turkey producers in the county that sell direct to consumers. Many farms are contract farms but a few independent producers still remain. Poultry and eggs are a great source of nutrition.

AN ASSORTMENT OF FOWL IS RAISED ON POULTRY FARMS. FOR MANY YEARS HENRY AND LEONA YOUNG MANAGED THE WALTER ANDREW'S FARM NEAR CHROME IN EAST NOTTINGHAM TOWNSHIP. THE SIGN IS FROM LOAG'S CORNER TURKEY FARM IN WEST NANTMEAL TOWNSHIP.

Fancy Chicken Log

16 ounces cream cheese, softened
1 tablespoon steak sauce
1/2 teaspoon curry powder
1 1/2 cups finely chopped cooked chicken
1/2 cup finely chopped celery

2 tablespoons chopped parsley
1/4 cup chopped nuts
2 tablespoons chopped parsley
Butter crackers

Beat the cream cheese, steak sauce and curry powder in a mixing bowl until smooth. Add the chicken, celery and 2 tablespoons parsley and mix well. Shape into a 9-inch log. Wrap in plastic wrap. Chill for 4 to 12 hours. Unwrap and sprinkle with the nuts and 2 tablespoons parsley. Serve with butter crackers.

Yield: 16 servings

Chicken Corn Soup

THIS SOUP IS SERVED AT MANY PUBLIC SALES AND CHURCH FUNCTIONS IN CHESTER COUNTY.

1 (3- to 4-pound) chicken
1 tablespoon salt
1/4 teaspoon pepper
1 1/2 cups chopped celery
1 medium onion, chopped
2 tablespoons chopped fresh parsley

4 cups whole kernel corn
6 ounces medium noodles, cooked, drained
Chopped fresh parsley
Chopped hard-cooked egg

Place the chicken in a large stockpot. Season with the salt and pepper. Add enough water to cover. Cook until the chicken is tender and falls from the bones. Remove the chicken from the stockpot, reserving the broth. Cut the chicken into small pieces, discarding the skin and bones. Bring the reserved broth to a boil. Add the celery, onion, 2 tablespoons parsley and corn. Cook for 15 minutes or until tender. Add the chicken and noodles. Cook until heated through. Ladle into soup bowls. Sprinkle with chopped fresh parsley and hard-cooked egg.

Yield: 6 to 8 servings

Curried Chicken and Green Bean Salad

SERVE THIS ELEGANT SALAD WITH CRUSTY FRENCH BREAD AND FRESH FRUIT.

12 ounces fresh green beans
Salt to taste
2 cups shredded cooked chicken
1 cup thinly sliced red onion
1/4 cup chopped fresh cilantro
1 teaspoon curry powder

1/3 cup plain nonfat yogurt
3 tablespoons reduced-fat mayonnaise
1 tablespoon fresh lime juice
Pepper to taste
2 tablespoons sliced almonds, toasted
1 tablespoon chopped fresh cilantro

Trim the green beans and snap into halves. Cook the green beans in boiling salted water in a saucepan for 3 to 5 minutes or until tender-crisp. Rinse immediately under cold running water to stop the cooking process; drain. Place in a large bowl. Add the chicken, red onion and 1/4 cup cilantro and toss to mix. Heat the curry powder in a small skillet over medium heat for 30 seconds or until aromatic, stirring constantly. Place in a small bowl. Add the yogurt, mayonnaise and lime juice and mix well. Add to the chicken mixture and toss to coat. Season with salt and pepper to taste. Sprinkle with the almonds and 1 tablespoon cilantro. You may prepare the salad 2 hours ahead of serving time and chill, covered, in the refrigerator.

Yield: 6 servings

Curried Chicken Salad

1 cup mayonnaise
1/2 to 1 teaspoon curry powder
2 cups chopped cooked chicken
1 cup chopped celery
1 (20-ounce) can chunk pineapple, drained
2 large bananas, sliced

1 (11-ounce) can mandarin oranges, drained
1/2 cup flaked coconut
Fresh salad greens, torn (optional)
3/4 cup peanuts or cashews

Mix the mayonnaise and curry powder in a small bowl. Combine with the chicken and celery in a large bowl and mix well. Chill, covered, for 30 minutes or longer. Add the pineapple, bananas, mandarin oranges and coconut and toss gently. Spoon over fresh salad greens on individual serving plates. Sprinkle with the peanuts.

Yield: 4 to 6 servings

Chicken Salad

    3 cups chopped cooked chicken breasts
    1 (11-ounce) can mandarin oranges, drained
    1 cup unsalted cashews
    1 cup green grape halves
    1 apple, peeled, chopped
    3/4 cup mayonnaise-type salad dressing
    1 tablespoon orange juice
    1/2 teaspoon curry powder

Combine the chicken, mandarin oranges, cashews, grapes and apple in a large bowl. Mix the mayonnaise-type salad dressing, orange juice and curry powder in a small bowl. Add to the chicken mixture and toss gently to mix. Chill, covered, in the refrigerator until serving time.

    Yield: 6 servings

Turkey Fruit Salad

    4 cups chopped cooked turkey
    1 cup pineapple tidbits
    1 cup seedless grapes
    1 cup chopped apples
    1 cup chopped walnuts
    1 1/2 cups mayonnaise

Combine the turkey, pineapple, grapes, apples and walnuts in a large bowl. Add the mayonnaise and toss gently to coat. Chill, covered, until serving time.

    Yield: 6 servings

White Chili

5 (16-ounce) cans assorted beans, such as Northern white beans,
   white lima beans, kidney beans and black-eyed peas
2 pounds boneless skinless chicken breasts
1 medium onion, chopped
2 garlic cloves, chopped
1 to 3 hot peppers (optional)
1 tablespoon vegetable oil
1 cup salsa
1 (29-ounce) can whole tomatoes, coarsely chopped
2 tablespoons chili powder
1 teaspoon salt
1 teaspoon pepper

Drain the beans, reserving ¹/₂ of the liquid. Cut the chicken into ¹/₂-inch pieces. Sauté the chicken, onion, garlic and hot peppers in the vegetable oil in a skillet until the chicken begins to brown. Add the salsa. Simmer for 5 to 10 minutes or until the liquid is reduced. Place in a 5-quart stockpot or slow cooker. Add the undrained tomatoes, beans and reserved liquid and mix well. Season with the chili powder, salt and pepper. Simmer for 2 to 3 hours or longer. Store, covered, in the refrigerator or freezer for 8 to 12 hours and reheat before serving for enhanced flavor.

Yield: 6 servings

Chicken à la Roma

1 (3- to 4-pound) chicken
1 (10-ounce) can cream of mushroom soup
1 (8-ounce) can tomato sauce
1 medium onion, chopped
1 teaspoon (heaping) basil
2 cups water
1 cup uncooked rice

Place the chicken in a large saucepan. Add the soup, tomato sauce, onion and basil. Simmer, covered, for 1 hour or until the chicken is cooked through. Bring the water to a boil in a saucepan. Add the rice and reduce the heat. Simmer, covered, for 15 minutes. Serve the chicken mixture over the hot cooked rice. You may cook the chicken mixture in a slow cooker on Low for 5 hours.

Yield: 4 to 6 servings

SPRINGTON MANOR FARM'S GREAT BARN HOUSES
A PETTING ZOO FOR CHILDREN.

Spicy Canadian Chicken

4 chicken leg quarters, or 8 chicken legs
Flour
Vegetable oil
1 cup cider vinegar
³/4 cup sugar
³/4 cup ketchup
1 garlic clove, minced
1 tablespoon Worcestershire sauce
1 tablespoon curry powder
1 teaspoon dry mustard
1 teaspoon paprika
1 teaspoon salt
¹/8 teaspoon pepper

Dredge the chicken in flour. Brown the chicken in vegetable oil in a skillet. Place in a baking dish. Combine the vinegar, sugar, ketchup, garlic, Worcestershire sauce, curry powder, dry mustard, paprika, salt and pepper in a saucepan and mix well. Bring to a boil and reduce the heat. Simmer for 5 minutes. Pour over the chicken. Bake, uncovered, at 350 degrees for 1 hour, turning the chicken after 30 minutes. Serve with hot parslied rice.

Yield: 4 servings

Basil Garlic Chicken

4 cups chicken broth
¹/₂ cup finely chopped fresh basil
3 tablespoons minced garlic cloves
2 tablespoons fresh gingerroot
Sea salt to taste
¹/₂ teaspoon freshly cracked pepper
6 boneless chicken breasts

Mix the chicken broth, basil, garlic, gingerroot, sea salt and pepper in a bowl and mix well. Pierce the chicken and place in a sealable plastic food storage bag. Add the broth mixture. Seal the bag. Marinate in the refrigerator for 2 to 12 hours.

Drain the chicken, reserving the marinade. Boil the reserved marinade in a saucepan for 2 to 3 minutes and remove from the heat. Place the chicken on a grill rack. Grill until the chicken is cooked through, turning and basting several times with the heated marinade. Serve with lemon wedges to squeeze over the chicken.

Yield: 6 servings

Chicken Salad Blitz

2 cups chopped Basil Garlic Chicken
¹/₂ cup grape halves or sliced apples
¹/₄ to ¹/₂ cup chopped celery
¹/₄ cup chopped onion
¹/₄ to ¹/₂ cup mayonnaise
Hot sauce to taste
Salt and pepper to taste

Combine Basil Garlic Chicken, grapes, celery and onion in a bowl. Add the mayonnaise, hot sauce, salt and pepper and toss gently to mix. Serve as a sandwich filling or use to stuff fresh tomatoes. You may add slivered almonds or pine nuts if desired.

Yield: 4 to 6 servings

Rosemary Chicken Breasts

JIM GERLACH, STATE SENATOR

> 5 garlic cloves, minced
> 2 tablespoons minced fresh rosemary, or 1 teaspoon dried rosemary
> 1 tablespoon Dijon mustard
> 1 tablespoon fresh lemon juice
> 3/4 teaspoon salt
> 1/4 teaspoon pepper
> 2 tablespoons olive oil
> 4 boneless skinless chicken breasts

Combine the garlic, rosemary, Dijon mustard, lemon juice, salt, pepper and olive oil in a bowl and mix well. Place the chicken in a shallow glass dish. Pour the garlic mixture over the chicken, turning the chicken to coat. Marinate, covered, at room temperature for 30 minutes, turning the chicken once or twice. Drain the chicken, reserving the marinade. Pour the reserved marinade into a small saucepan. Boil for 2 to 3 minutes, stirring frequently. Place the chicken on a grill rack. Grill 4 to 6 inches from the hot coals for 8 to 10 minutes or until the chicken tests done, turning once and basting with the heated marinade.

Yield: 4 servings

SPRINGTON MANOR FARM'S GREAT BARN IN
WALLACE TOWNSHIP STILL RETAINS ITS HYDRAULIC
RAM SYSTEM CISTERN.

Sesame Chicken with Cumberland Sauce

1 cup bread crumbs
1/4 cup plus 2 tablespoons sesame seeds
1/4 cup grated Parmesan cheese
2 tablespoons chopped fresh parsley
1/4 teaspoon white pepper
8 large boneless chicken breasts
1/4 cup (1/2 stick) margarine, melted
Cumberland Sauce

Combine the bread crumbs, sesame seeds, Parmesan cheese, parsley and white pepper in a medium bowl and mix well. Dip the chicken in the margarine. Coat with the bread crumb mixture. Place in a baking dish. Bake at 425 degrees for 20 minutes or until the chicken tests done. Place the chicken on a serving plate. Spoon some of the Cumberland Sauce over the chicken. Serve with the remaining Cumberland Sauce.

Yield: 8 servings

Cumberland Sauce

1 orange
2 teaspoons cornstarch
1 teaspoon Dijon mustard
1/8 teaspoon ginger
1/8 teaspoon red pepper
1 tablespoon lemon juice
1/3 cup red currant jelly

Remove the peel from the orange with a vegetable peeler. Cut into julienne strips. Place in a 1-quart saucepan. Add enough cold water to cover. Bring to a boil; drain. Repeat twice.

Cut the orange into halves. Squeeze enough juice into a glass measuring cup to equal 1/2 cup. Combine the cornstarch, Dijon mustard, ginger and red pepper in a saucepan and mix until smooth. Stir in the orange juice, lemon juice and jelly. The mixture will be lumpy. Cook over medium heat until slightly thickened, stirring constantly. Boil for 1 minute. Remove from the heat. Stir in the blanched orange peel.

Yield: 1 cup sauce

Sautéed Chicken Cutlets

¹/₄ cup flour
¹/₄ teaspoon salt
¹/₈ teaspoon pepper
4 boneless skinless chicken breasts
3 tablespoons butter or margarine

8 ounces fresh mushrooms, sliced
1 small onion, chopped
³/₄ cup chicken broth
¹/₂ cup vermouth or dry white wine
Chopped fresh parsley

Combine the flour, salt and pepper in a plastic food storage bag and shake to mix well. Add the chicken and shake to coat. Cook the chicken in the butter in a 10-inch skillet over medium heat for 10 minutes or until the chicken is brown and cooked through. Remove the chicken to a serving platter and keep warm. Add the mushrooms and onion to the hot drippings in the skillet. Sauté over medium heat until the onion is translucent and the liquid is evaporated. Stir in the chicken broth and vermouth. Bring to a boil and reduce the heat to low. Simmer for 5 minutes or until the sauce is slightly thickened, stirring occasionally. Spoon over the chicken. Sprinkle with parsley.

Yield: 4 servings

MASONRY CONICAL COLUMNS CAN BE FOUND ON
NUMEROUS HISTORIC CHESTER COUNTY STONE BARNS.

Stuffed Chicken Breasts Tarragon

8 ounces fresh mushrooms, finely chopped
3 green onions, chopped
1/2 teaspoon crushed tarragon leaves
1 tablespoon butter or margarine
2 tablespoons dry sherry
1/4 cup soft bread crumbs
1/4 teaspoon salt
4 chicken breasts
2 tablespoons butter or margarine, softened
Paprika to taste

Sauté the mushrooms, green onions and tarragon in 1 tablespoon butter in a 10-inch skillet over medium heat until the mushrooms are tender. Add the sherry. Cook until the liquid is evaporated, stirring occasionally. Stir in the bread crumbs and salt.

Cut a slit lengthwise in the thickest part of each chicken breast to form a pocket. Spoon the mushroom mixture into each pocket. Arrange the chicken skin side up in an 8×12-inch baking dish. Spread the chicken with 2 tablespoons butter. Sprinkle with paprika. Bake at 400 degrees for 30 minutes or until the chicken is cooked through.

Yield: 4 servings

Chicken Supreme

2 boneless skinless chicken breasts, partially frozen
1 (10-ounce) can cream of chicken soup
1 tomato, sliced
2 ounces Swiss cheese, sliced
1/2 cup lightly buttered bread crumbs

Cut the chicken into thin slices. Place in an 8-inch greased baking dish. Cover with the soup. Arrange the tomato and Swiss cheese over the soup. Sprinkle with the bread crumbs. Bake at 350 degrees for 35 minutes or until the chicken is cooked through. Serve with hot cooked rice.

Yield: 2 servings

Chicken and Stuffing Casserole

1 (7-ounce) package herb stuffing mix
1/2 cup (1 stick) butter, melted
1 cup chicken broth
1 (10-ounce) can cream of mushroom soup
1 (8-ounce) can sliced mushrooms
3/4 cup mayonnaise
1/4 cup light cream
1/4 teaspoon paprika
1/8 teaspoon nutmeg
3 cups chopped cooked chicken

Combine the stuffing mix, butter and chicken broth in a bowl and mix well. Combine the soup, undrained mushrooms, mayonnaise and cream in a saucepan and mix well. Cook until heated through. Season with paprika and nutmeg. Place the chicken in a 9×12-inch baking dish. Pour the mushroom mixture over the chicken. Top with the stuffing mixture. Bake at 350 degrees for 30 minutes.

Yield: 8 servings

Chicken Enchiladas

1 large onion, chopped
2 hot peppers, chopped
2 green bell peppers, chopped
1 (16-ounce) can tomatoes, chopped
1 teaspoon salt
4 boneless skinless chicken breasts, cooked, chopped
2 cups sour cream
1 (3-ounce) can pitted black olives, drained, sliced
8 ounces Monterey Jack cheese, shredded
8 ounces longhorn cheese, shredded
1 (10-count) package white flour tortillas

Combine the onion, hot peppers, bell peppers, tomatoes and salt in a saucepan. Bring to a boil and reduce the heat. Simmer until the vegetables are tender. Combine the chicken, 1 cup of the salsa, 1 cup of the sour cream, black olives, $1/2$ of the Monterey Jack cheese and $1/2$ of the longhorn cheese in a bowl and mix well. Spread over each tortilla and roll up. Place in a large baking dish. Sprinkle with the remaining Monterey Jack and longhorn cheese. Bake at 350 degrees until heated through and the cheese is melted. Serve with the remaining salsa and sour cream. You may use prepared salsa if desired.

Yield: 10 servings

A CHICKEN HOUSE DISTINGUISHES A POULTRY
FARM ON KINGS HIGHWAY, ROUTE #340,
IN WEST CALN TOWNSHIP.

Creamy Chicken Lasagna

2 (10-ounce) cans cream of mushroom soup
1 1/2 cups milk
1/8 teaspoon nutmeg
1/8 teaspoon ground red pepper or cayenne pepper
1 (10-ounce) package frozen chopped spinach, thawed, drained
1 egg
15 ounces ricotta cheese
12 lasagna noodles, cooked, drained
1 1/3 cups shredded mozzarella cheese
2 cups chopped cooked chicken
2/3 cup shredded mozzarella cheese
1/2 cup grated Parmesan cheese

Mix the soup, milk, nutmeg and red pepper in a bowl. Combine the spinach, egg and ricotta cheese in a bowl and mix well. Spread 1/2 cup of the soup mixture in a 9×13-inch baking dish. Arrange 4 of the noodles over the soup mixture. Reserve 1/2 cup of the remaining soup mixture. Layer the remaining soup mixture, spinach mixture, 1 1/3 cups mozzarella cheese, chicken and remaining noodles 1/2 at a time over the layers. Spread the reserved soup mixture over the top. Sprinkle with 2/3 cup mozzarella cheese and Parmesan cheese. Bake at 350 degrees for 40 minutes or until hot and bubbly. Let stand for 15 minutes before serving.

Yield: 8 servings

Chicken Corn Pie

1 (2-crust) pie pastry
4 boneless skinless chicken breasts,
  cooked, chopped
4 large potatoes, cooked, peeled, cubed
1/2 large onion, thinly sliced

1 (16-ounce) can whole kernel corn,
  drained
Salt and pepper to taste
2 tablespoons butter
1/4 cup milk

Line a 10-inch pie plate with 1 of the pie pastries. Combine the chicken, potatoes, onion, corn, salt and pepper in a bowl and mix well. Spoon into the prepared pie plate. Dot with the butter. Pour the milk over the filling. Top with the remaining pie pastry, sealing and fluting the edge and cutting vents. Bake at 375 degrees for 45 minutes or until the pastry is golden brown.

Yield: 6 to 8 servings

Parsley Pinwheel Potpie

1 (3-pound) chicken
1 teaspoon salt
Flour
4 medium potatoes, quartered
2 cups flour

1 tablespoon baking powder
1 teaspoon salt
1/4 cup shortening
1/2 cup (about) milk
2 tablespoons chopped parsley

Combine the chicken and 1 teaspoon salt with enough water to cover in a saucepan. Bring to a boil and reduce the heat. Simmer until the chicken is cooked through. Drain the chicken, reserving the stock. Cut the chicken into pieces, discarding the skin and bones. Bring the reserved stock to a boil in a saucepan. Add enough flour to make of a gravy consistency. Cook until thickened, stirring constantly. Cook the potatoes in water to cover for 10 minutes; drain. Mix 2 cups flour, baking powder and 1 teaspoon salt in a bowl. Cut in the shortening until crumbly. Add enough milk to form a soft dough. Knead on a lightly floured surface until smooth. Roll into a rectangle 1/8 inch thick. Sprinkle the parsley over the dough and roll up as for a jellyroll. Cut into 1 1/2- to 2-inch pieces. Layer the chicken and potatoes in a baking dish. Add enough of the gravy to cover. Arrange the dough pieces cut side down on the top. Bake at 425 degrees for 25 minutes or until the top is golden brown.

Yield: 6 to 8 servings

Duck with Orange Sauce

1 (12-ounce) jar orange marmalade
Ginger to taste
1 teaspoon hot mustard, or to taste
Worcestershire sauce to taste
Orange juice
2 (4¹/₂- to 5-pound) mallard ducks
Apple slices

Combine the orange marmalade, ginger, hot mustard and Worcestershire sauce in a bowl and mix well. Add enough orange juice to make of a sauce consistency.

Stuff the duck cavities with apple slices. Place in an oven-cooking bag. Add the orange marmalade mixture. Bake at 325 degrees for about 1¹/₄ to 1¹/₂ hours (25 minutes per pound) or until the ducks are cooked through. Remove the ducks and cut into slices. Serve with the sauce.

Yield: 4 servings

Vegetables AND Herbs

SPONSOR: CHESTER-DELAWARE POMONA GRANGE #3

The bountiful pumpkin harvest is featured at the farmstead of Glen Willow Orchards, Avondale.

From its founding in 1867, the purpose of the grange has been to build higher manhood and womanhood in the rural community. Chester-Delaware Pomona Grange #3 has carried out the Grange mission in Chester County since 1874. Chester County farmers are among those who have benefitted from Grange programs and legislative policies.

Grange members have always been community oriented and help make Chester County an agricultural leader in the Commonwealth. Local Granges, such as Kennett, Brandywine, Russellville, London Grove, Goshen, East Lynn, Marshallton, Kimberton, Chester Valley, Honey Brook, and North Coventry meet regularly. Their members are the same ones who till the soil, maintain active dairy herds, and raise cash crops. Mushrooms,

fruit, vegetables, and flowers are all produced on these farms, which use the latest in scientific and technological innovations. This all contributes to the natural beauty of Chester County and diversifies the county's economy.

Youth may join Junior Grange at age five. Pennsylvania Grange Youth have opportunities for achieving in the merit badge program through the year and to participate in the annual Junior Camp.

The Order of Patrons of Husbandry is the world's oldest family agricultural fraternity. Grange ritual teaches that it is in the home that the farmer enjoys the fruits of his labors. As the farmer seeks new ideas to advance his profession, so the farm wife learns about new methods and improved products. Many recipes in this book are from those industrious women.

SPRINGTON MANOR FARM'S PERENNIAL GARDEN IN WALLACE TOWNSHIP WOULD NOT BE COMPLETE WITHOUT HERBS. MANY FARMERS CONTINUE THE TRADITION OF TRUCK FARMING THAT CONTAIN VARIOUS VEGETABLES AND HERBS. AUTUMN GETS DRESSED WITH ITS FINEST COLORS.

Spinach Dip in Loaf of Bread

1 (10-ounce) package frozen chopped spinach, thawed
1 1/2 cups sour cream
1 cup mayonnaise
1 envelope vegetable soup mix
1 (8-ounce) can water chestnuts, finely chopped
1 large round loaf bread

Squeeze excess moisture from the spinach. Combine the spinach, sour cream, mayonnaise, soup mix and water chestnuts in a bowl and mix well. Chill, covered, for 2 hours. Hollow out the bread to form a shell, reserving the bread center. Cut the bread center into cubes. Stir the spinach dip and spoon into the bread shell. Serve with the reserved bread cubes for dipping.

Yield: 3 cups dip

Spinach Balls

1 (10-ounce) package frozen chopped spinach
1 cup crushed herb-seasoned stuffing mix
1/3 cup grated Parmesan cheese
3 eggs, beaten
1 onion, chopped (optional)
1/4 cup (1/2 stick) butter, melted

Cook the spinach using the package directions; drain. Combine the spinach, stuffing mix, Parmesan cheese, eggs, onion and butter in a bowl and mix well. Roll the mixture into 1-inch balls. Place on an ungreased baking sheet. Bake at 350 degrees for 10 minutes. You may freeze the unbaked spinach balls and store in freezer bags until needed. Bake the frozen unbaked spinach balls at 350 degrees for 20 minutes.

Yield: 50 spinach balls

Poor Man's Caviar

1 (2-pound) eggplant
1 cup finely chopped onions
1/4 cup olive oil
1/2 cup finely chopped green bell pepper
1 teaspoon finely chopped garlic
2 large tomatoes, peeled, seeded, finely chopped, or 1/4 cup canned tomato purée
1/2 teaspoon sugar
2 teaspoons salt
Freshly ground pepper to taste
2 tablespoons olive oil
2 to 3 tablespoons lemon juice
Salt to taste

Place the eggplant on a rack in a baking pan. Bake at 425 degrees for 1 hour or until the eggplant is soft and the skin is charred and blistered, turning once or twice. Let cool. Sauté the onions in 1/4 cup olive oil in a skillet over medium heat for 6 to 8 minutes or until tender but not brown. Stir in the bell pepper and garlic. Cook for 5 minutes, stirring occasionally. Scrape the entire contents of the skillet into a mixing bowl.

Remove the skin from the eggplant using a small sharp knife. Chop the eggplant finely until almost puréed. Add the eggplant, tomatoes, sugar, 2 teaspoons salt and pepper to taste to the sautéed vegetables in the mixing bowl and mix well. Heat 2 tablespoons olive oil in a skillet over medium heat. Add the eggplant mixture. Bring to a boil, stirring constantly. Reduce the heat to low. Simmer, covered, for 1 hour. Cook, uncovered, for 30 minutes longer or until all of the moisture is evaporated and the mixture is thick enough to hold its shape in a spoon, stirring frequently. Stir in 2 tablespoons of the lemon juice. Season with additional salt, pepper and lemon juice to taste if needed. Place in a bowl. Chill, covered with plastic wrap, until ready to serve. Serve with pumpernickel bread squares or sesame seed crackers.

Yield: 3 cups dip

Black Bean and Corn Salsa

1 (16-ounce) can black beans, rinsed, drained
3/4 cup whole kernel corn
2 medium tomatoes, chopped
4 green onions, thinly sliced
2 tablespoons finely chopped fresh cilantro
1 tablespoon red wine vinegar
1/2 teaspoon sugar
1/2 teaspoon cumin
1/8 teaspoon oregano, or to taste
1/8 teaspoon cayenne pepper
1/8 teaspoon freshly ground black pepper
Salt to taste

Combine the black beans, corn, tomatoes, green onions, cilantro, red wine vinegar, sugar, cumin, oregano, cayenne pepper, black pepper and salt to taste in a bowl and mix well. Chill, covered, in the refrigerator.

Yield: 4 cups dip

Garden Bruschetta

2 cups finely chopped tomatoes
1/3 cup finely chopped fresh basil
1 tablespoon minced fresh garlic
2 teaspoons balsamic vinegar
Salt and cracked pepper to taste
1 French baguette
Olive oil

Combine the tomatoes, basil, garlic, balsamic vinegar, salt and pepper in a bowl and mix well. Chill, covered, in the refrigerator for 1 hour. Cut the baguette diagonally into slices 1/2 inch thick. Brush with olive oil. Place on a baking sheet. Broil until light brown on each side, turning once. Spoon the tomato mixture over the top.

Yield: 12 servings

Tapenade

2 cups mayonnaise or reduced-fat mayonnaise
1 (7-ounce) can tuna, drained
1 1/2 anchovy fillets, or 1 teaspoon anchovy paste
3 tablespoons chopped black olives
1 scallion, chopped
1/4 cup chopped onion
2 garlic cloves
1/4 cup cream of potato soup or instant mashed potatoes
1/2 teaspoon Worcestershire sauce
1/8 teaspoon Tabasco sauce

Process the mayonnaise, tuna, anchovies, black olives, scallion, onion, garlic, soup, Worcestershire sauce and Tabasco sauce in a food processor or blender until smooth. Spoon into a serving bowl. Chill, covered, in the refrigerator. Serve with assorted Chester County vegetables and pumpernickel rye or party rounds.

Yield: 2 cups dip

THE POPULAR AMISH PLACE FARM PRODUCE
STAND IS LOCATED ON LINCOLN HIGHWAY,
BUSINESS ROUTE #30, IN CALN TOWNSHIP.

Sweet-and-Sour Cabbage Soup

6 cups vegetable broth or beef broth
1³/₄ pounds green cabbage, quartered, cored, thinly shredded
1 (9-ounce) sweet onion, cut into halves, cut into thin strips
¹/₂ cup dried cherries, cranberries or raisins
1 (16-ounce) can whole tomatoes, drained, seeded, cut into strips
1 pound boneless beef chuck cubes for stew
¹/₂ teaspoon pepper
¹/₃ cup sugar
¹/₄ cup fresh lemon juice
2 tablespoons snipped fresh dill
1 teaspoon salt
Fresh dill sprigs

Bring the broth to a boil in a saucepan. Remove from the heat. Layer the cabbage, onion, dried cherries and tomatoes in a 5- or 6-quart slow cooker. Place the beef over the layers and season with pepper. Add the hot broth. Cook, covered, on Low for 9 to 10 hours or on High for 4¹/₂ to 5 hours or until the vegetables are tender. Combine the sugar, lemon juice, dill and salt in a small bowl and whisk well. Stir into the soup. Let stand for 15 minutes. Ladle into soup bowls. Garnish with fresh dill sprigs.

Yield: 8 servings

Pumpkin Leek Soup

TERRACE RESTAURANT, LONGWOOD GARDENS

2¹/2 cups chopped leeks (white part only)
2 tablespoons vegetable oil
1 (29-ounce) can mashed cooked
    pumpkin
1 (10-ounce) can vegetable broth or
    reduced-sodium chicken broth
1 teaspoon cinnamon
¹/2 teaspoon nutmeg

¹/2 teaspoon ginger
1 teaspoon allspice
¹/4 teaspoon cloves (optional)
Salt and pepper to taste
¹/4 cup heavy cream
¹/4 cup sliced almonds, toasted
Sour cream

Sauté the leeks in the vegetable oil in a large saucepan over medium heat until tender. Add the pumpkin, vegetable broth, cinnamon, nutmeg, ginger, allspice and cloves and mix well. Cover and reduce the heat. Simmer for 20 minutes. Process in a blender or food processor until blended; do not overblend. Return to the saucepan. Season with salt and pepper to taste. Add the cream. Cook until heated through; do not boil. Ladle into soup bowls. Sprinkle with the almonds and add a dollop of sour cream.

Yield: 6 to 8 servings

A BOUNTIFUL HARVEST OF PUMPKINS AT
AMISH PLACE IN CALN TOWNSHIP.

Spicy Butternut Squash Soup

3³/4 pounds butternut squash (about 2 medium)
2 tablespoons olive oil
5 cups (or more) chicken stock or reduced-sodium broth
1¹/2 teaspoons minced jalapeño chiles
Salt to taste
Jalapeño chile rings to taste
¹/8 teaspoon saffron threads

Peel the squash. Cut each squash lengthwise into halves. Scoop out the seeds. Cut enough of the squash into thin slices to measure 1 cup. Cut the remaining squash into 1-inch pieces. Sauté the squash slices in the olive oil in a large heavy skillet over medium-high heat for 8 minutes or until brown. Place in a large heavy stockpot. Add the remaining squash, 5 cups chicken stock and minced jalapeño chiles. Bring to a boil and reduce the heat.

Simmer for 25 minutes or until the squash is very tender. Purée in batches in a blender. Return to the stockpot. Season with salt. Return to a simmer, adding additional stock if needed for the desired consistency. Stir in jalapeño chile rings to taste and saffron. Simmer for 2 minutes. Ladle into serving bowls.

Yield: 6 servings

Fresh Tomato Soup

2 cups chopped fresh tomatoes
1/4 cup chopped onion
1 bay leaf
1/2 teaspoon sugar

Salt and pepper to taste
2 tablespoons butter
2 tablespoons flour
2 cups milk

Combine the tomatoes, onion, bay leaf, sugar, salt and pepper in a saucepan and mix well. Bring to a boil and reduce the heat. Simmer for 10 minutes. Press through a sieve into a bowl, discarding the solids. Melt the butter in the saucepan. Stir in the flour and salt. Add the milk. Cook until thickened, stirring constantly. Stir in the hot tomato mixture gradually. Ladle into soup bowls. Garnish with snipped green onion tops.

Yield: 4 servings

Caesar Salad

2 tablespoons coarsely chopped garlic
Juice of 2 lemons
1 large anchovy
1 tablespoon Dijon mustard
1 tablespoon cider vinegar
6 to 8 ounces olive oil
3 dashes of Tabasco sauce
3 dashes of Worcestershire sauce

1/4 cup freshly grated Parmesan cheese
1/8 teaspoon salt
Freshly cracked pepper to taste
Hearts of romaine
Freshly grated Parmesan cheese
  to taste
Croutons

Process the garlic, lemon juice, anchovy, Dijon mustard and cider vinegar in a food processor. Add the olive oil in a fine stream, processing constantly until emulsified. Add the Tabasco sauce, Worcestershire sauce, 1/4 cup Parmesan cheese, salt and pepper to taste and pulse a few times to blend. Combine the romaine, Parmesan cheese to taste, pepper to taste and croutons in a salad bowl. Drizzle with the salad dressing and toss to coat.

Yield: variable

Mandarin Almond Salad

1/4 cup sliced almonds
4 1/2 teaspoons sugar
1/4 head iceberg lettuce, rinsed, chilled
1/4 head romaine, rinsed, chilled
1 cup chopped celery (optional)
2 green onions with tops, thinly sliced
Vinaigrette
1 (11-ounce) can mandarin oranges, drained

Cook the almonds and sugar in a skillet over low heat until the sugar melts and coats the almonds, stirring constantly. Remove from the heat and cool. Break apart and store at room temperature. Tear the lettuce and romaine into bite-size pieces. Combine with the celery and green onions in a sealable plastic food storage bag. Seal and store in the refrigerator for up to 24 hours.

To serve, pour the Vinaigrette over the salad green mixture in the bag. Add the mandarin oranges and sugar-coated almonds. Seal the bag and shake to coat.

Yield: 4 to 6 servings

Vinaigrette

1/4 cup salad oil
2 tablespoons vinegar
1 tablespoon snipped parsley
1/2 teaspoon salt
1/8 teaspoon black pepper
1/8 teaspoon red pepper sauce

Combine the salad oil, vinegar, parsley, salt, black pepper and red pepper sauce in a jar with a tight-fitting lid. Seal the jar and shake to mix well. Store, tightly covered, until ready to serve.

Yield: about 1/2 cup vinaigrette

Spinach Apricot Salad

1 cup boiling water
6 ounces dried apricot halves
10 ounces fresh spinach, trimmed
3 tablespoons cider vinegar
3 tablespoons apricot preserves
1/2 cup vegetable oil
1/2 cup macadamia nuts, coarsely chopped, toasted

Pour the boiling water over the apricots in a heatproof bowl. Let stand for 30 minutes; drain. Rinse the spinach and pat dry. Tear into bite-size pieces. Process the vinegar and preserves in a blender until smooth, stopping once to scrape down the sides. Add the oil in a fine steady stream, processing constantly at high speed.

Combine the spinach, 1/2 of the apricots, 1/2 of the macadamia nuts and the dressing in a salad bowl and toss gently to coat. Sprinkle with the remaining apricot halves and macadamia nuts. Serve immediately.

Yield: 8 servings

THE 1910 ICE HARVEST REQUIRED EXTENSIVE
HORSEPOWER AND MANPOWER AT
VALLEY BROOK FARM, CALN TOWNSHIP.

Spinach Salad

8 dried green or black figs, chopped
7 ounces baby spinach
1 yellow bell pepper, thinly sliced
1 red bell pepper, thinly sliced
1/4 cup thinly sliced red onion
1/4 cup feta cheese
1/4 cup chopped pecans, toasted

3 tablespoons olive oil
1 tablespoon lemon juice
1/4 teaspoon minced garlic
1/4 teaspoon honey
1/4 teaspoon pepper
4 fresh basil leaves, chopped

Combine the figs, spinach, bell peppers, onion, feta cheese and pecans in a salad bowl and toss to mix well. Combine the olive oil, lemon juice, garlic, honey, pepper and basil in a jar with a tight-fitting lid. Cover and shake to blend well. Pour over the salad and toss to coat. Serve immediately.

Yield: 6 servings

Mandarin Orange Spinach Salad

ELINOR Z. TAYLOR, STATE REPRESENTATIVE

1/2 cup cider vinegar
1/2 cup water
3/4 cup sugar
1 teaspoon salt
1 egg, beaten
1 (7-ounce) package fresh spinach leaves,
   trimmed, torn into bite-size pieces

1 (11-ounce) can mandarin
   oranges, drained
1/2 cup chopped red onion
2 hard-cooked eggs, chopped
1 cup sliced fresh Pennsylvania
   mushrooms
6 slices cooked bacon, crumbled

Bring the vinegar, water, sugar and salt to a boil in a saucepan. Boil until the sugar is dissolved, stirring constantly. Remove from the heat. Stir a small amount of the hot mixture into the beaten egg. Stir the beaten egg into the hot mixture. Chill, covered, in the refrigerator. Combine the spinach, mandarin oranges, onion, hard-cooked eggs, mushrooms and bacon in a large salad bowl and toss to mix well. Add the desired amount of dressing and toss to coat.

Yield: 4 servings

Strawberry Spinach Salad

8 cups torn spinach
2 cups sliced fresh strawberries
$1/3$ cup vegetable oil
2 tablespoons cider vinegar
2 tablespoons strawberry jam

Toss the spinach and strawberries in a salad bowl. Mix the vegetable oil, vinegar and jam in a bowl. Pour over the spinach mixture and toss to coat. You may add $1/2$ cup sliced green onions or 1 cup chopped toasted pecans if desired.

Yield: 6 servings

Great-Grandmother's Coleslaw

1 medium head cabbage
Salt to taste
$2/3$ cup sugar
$1^1/2$ cups milk
White vinegar
Nutmeg to taste

Shred the cabbage. Drain in a colander. Sprinkle with salt to draw out the water. Let stand for 2 hours to drain. Squeeze the cabbage to remove as much moisture as possible. Place in a large bowl.

Dissolve the sugar in the milk in a bowl. Add enough vinegar to thicken the mixture. Pour over the cabbage and toss lightly to mix. Sprinkle with nutmeg.

Yield: 6 to 8 servings

Oriental Slaw

2 (3-ounce) packages beef-flavor ramen noodles
1/3 cup cider vinegar or balsamic vinegar
3/4 cup vegetable oil
1/2 cup sugar
16 ounces coleslaw mix
3 green onions, thinly sliced
1 cup sunflower seed kernels, toasted
1 cup sliced almonds, toasted

Crumble the noodles, reserving the seasoning packets. Mix the vinegar, vegetable oil, sugar and reserved seasoning in a bowl. Let stand for several hours. Combine the coleslaw mix, green onions, crumbled noodles, sunflower seed kernels and almonds in a bowl and toss to mix well. Add the dressing and toss to coat. Serve immediately or chill, covered, until serving time. You may add chopped cooked ham, chicken or turkey for a main dish salad.

Yield: 12 servings

CUTTING ICE WAS ALWAYS A VERY COLD CHORE.

Fresh Tomato and Mozzarella Salad

4 large fresh tomatoes, sliced
4 (1-ounce) balls fresh mozzarella cheese, sliced
12 fresh basil leaves, torn
Salt and freshly ground pepper to taste
1/4 cup Italian Salad Dressing

Arrange the tomatoes on a salad plate. Cover the tomatoes with the mozzarella cheese. Sprinkle with the basil, salt and pepper. Drizzle with the salad dressing. Serve with fresh Italian bread.

Yield: 4 servings

Italian Salad Dressing

1/2 cup olive oil
1/2 cup vegetable or canola oil
1/2 cup wine vinegar
1 teaspoon salt
1 teaspoon sugar
1/2 teaspoon oregano
1 teaspoon dry mustard
1/2 teaspoon onion salt
1/2 teaspoon paprika
1/2 teaspoon garlic powder
1/8 teaspoon thyme

Combine the olive oil, vegetable or canola oil, wine vinegar, salt, sugar, oregano, dry mustard, onion salt, paprika, garlic powder and thyme in a jar with a tight-fitting lid. Cover the jar tightly and shake to mix well. Let stand for 2 hours for the flavors to blend. Shake before using.

Yield: 1 1/2 cups salad dressing

Crunchy Vegetable Salad

1 small head cauliflower
1 large bunch broccoli
2 small zucchini
3 carrots, thinly sliced
1 onion, finely chopped
$1/3$ cup chopped celery
$2/3$ cup mayonnaise
$1/3$ cup vegetable oil
3 tablespoons vinegar
$1/3$ cup sugar
1 teaspoon salt

Cut the cauliflower and broccoli into small florets. Cut the zucchini into halves lengthwise. Cut each half into thin slices. Combine the cauliflower, broccoli, zucchini, carrots, onion and celery in a large bowl. Mix the mayonnaise, vegetable oil, vinegar, sugar and salt in a small bowl. Add to the vegetable mixture and mix well. Chill, covered, for several hours before serving. You may add crumbled cooked bacon, black olives or mushrooms if desired.

Yield: 8 to 12 servings

Poached Egg with Asparagus

1 cup water
1/2 teaspoon salt
1 pound fresh asparagus, cut into 1-inch pieces
1 cup milk
2 eggs
2 slices bread, toasted

Bring the water and salt to a boil in a saucepan. Add the asparagus. Cook for 5 minutes or until tender; drain. Add the milk. Bring to a boil and reduce the heat to a simmer. Break the eggs carefully on top of the simmering asparagus. Cover and cook for 3 minutes or until the eggs are set. Place a poached egg in the center of each toast slice and surround with the asparagus.

Yield: 2 servings

RUSSELLVILLE GRANGE WAS THE COMMUNITY
CENTER FOR MANY DECADES IN THE UPPER OXFORD
TOWNSHIP VILLAGE OF THE SAME NAME.

Marinated Asparagus

8 ounces asparagus, trimmed
3 tablespoons red wine vinegar or balsamic vinegar
1 tablespoon dark sesame oil
1 tablespoon sesame seeds, toasted

Bring water to a boil in a saucepan. Add the asparagus. Cook for several minutes or until tender-crisp. Remove from the heat and place in a pan of ice water to stop the cooking process; drain. Mix the red wine vinegar, sesame oil and sesame seeds in a sealable plastic bag. Add the asparagus and seal the bag. Shake to coat well. Marinate in the refrigerator for 2 hours or up to several days before serving.

Yield: 4 servings

Baked Beans

1 pound dried Great Northern beans or navy beans
1/2 onion, minced
1 cup packed brown sugar
3 tablespoons ketchup
2 tablespoons molasses
2 tablespoons bacon drippings
1 teaspoon prepared mustard
1 teaspoon salt
1/4 teaspoon paprika
1/4 teaspoon pepper
4 to 8 ounces salt pork, sliced, or sliced bacon

Rinse and sort the beans. Soak the beans in water to cover in a saucepan for 8 to 12 hours; drain. Cook the beans in water to cover in a saucepan until tender. Drain, reserving the liquid. Combine the drained beans, onion, brown sugar, ketchup, molasses, bacon drippings, mustard, salt, paprika and pepper in a bowl and mix well. Pour into a baking dish. Place the salt pork on top. Bake at 325 degrees for 2 hours, adding the reserved liquid as needed for the desired consistency.

Yield: 6 to 8 servings

Pennsylvania Dutch Pickled Beets and Eggs

2 (16-ounce) cans tiny whole beets
1 small onion (optional)
8 hard-cooked eggs, peeled
1 cup sugar
3/4 cup apple cider vinegar
1 1/2 teaspoons salt
1/8 teaspoon pepper
2 bay leaves
12 whole cloves

Drain the beets, reserving 1 cup of the liquid. Cut the onion into halves. Cut each half into thinly sliced half-moons. Combine the beets, onion and hard-cooked eggs in a nonreactive or plastic container. Combine the sugar, reserved beet liquid, vinegar, salt, pepper, bay leaves and cloves in a medium nonreactive saucepan. Bring to a boil and reduce the heat. Simmer for 5 minutes. Pour over the beet mixture. Cool to room temperature. Cover and chill in the refrigerator for 48 hours before serving. Remove the bay leaves and whole cloves before serving.

Yield: 8 servings

Sweet-and-Sour Red Cabbage

1 head red cabbage, quartered, cored
1/2 cup red wine vinegar
1/2 teaspoon cinnamon
1/2 teaspoon ground cloves
1/4 teaspoon nutmeg
2 bay leaves
1/3 cup sugar
2 teaspoons salt
1/2 teaspoon white pepper
1 apple, peeled, sliced
1 onion, sliced
1 shot or jigger of red wine or water (1 to 2 ounces)
1 small potato, grated

Shred the cabbage and place in a large bowl. Combine the red wine vinegar, cinnamon, cloves, nutmeg, bay leaves, sugar, salt and white pepper in a bowl and mix well. Pour over the cabbage. Marinate, covered, in the refrigerator for 8 to 12 hours. Sauté the apple and onion in a large nonstick skillet over high heat until wilted. Add the undrained cabbage and red wine. Cook for 45 minutes, stirring frequently. Add the potato. Cook until thickened, stirring constantly. Remove the bay leaves.

Yield: 8 to 10 servings

THE FORMER EAST GOSHEN GRANGE ON
CHESTER ROAD, ROUTE #352.

Baked Corn

2 cups corn
1 cup milk
$^1/_4$ cup sugar
3 eggs
1 tablespoon cornstarch
1 teaspoon salt
$^1/_4$ teaspoon pepper
2 tablespoons butter

Process the corn, milk, sugar, eggs, cornstarch, salt, pepper and butter in a blender until blended. Pour into a greased 1$^1/_2$-quart baking dish. Bake at 350 degrees for 1 hour or until firm in the center. You may double this recipe if desired.

Yield: 4 servings

Vidalia Onion Pie

5 medium Vidalia onions, sliced
$^1/_2$ cup (1 stick) butter or margarine
3 eggs, beaten
1 cup sour cream
Tabasco sauce to taste
$^1/_4$ teaspoon dry mustard
$^1/_4$ teaspoon salt
$^1/_4$ teaspoon pepper
1 unbaked (9-inch) deep-dish pie shell
$^1/_2$ cup grated sharp Cheddar cheese

Sauté the onions in the butter in a skillet until translucent but not brown. Combine the eggs, sour cream, Tabasco sauce, dry mustard, salt and pepper in a medium bowl and mix well. Stir in the sautéed onions. Pour into the pie shell. Sprinkle with the cheese. Bake at 450 degrees for 20 minutes. Reduce the oven temperature to 325 degrees. Bake for 20 minutes longer or until the filling is set and the top is golden brown. Cool for 10 minutes before serving.

Yield: 6 to 8 servings

Tomato Tart

3 large tomatoes, cut into 1/2-inch slices
Salt to taste
1 1/2 cups flour
1/2 teaspoon salt
1/4 cup (1/2 stick) chilled unsalted butter, cut into small pieces
3 to 4 tablespoons cold water
2 tablespoons Dijon mustard
3 tablespoons chopped fresh basil
4 ounces mozzarella cheese, cut into 8 thin slices
1 cup whipping cream
2 eggs
Freshly ground pepper to taste

Sprinkle the tomatoes with salt to taste and place in a colander. Drain for 30 minutes. Remove the seeds. Pat the tomatoes dry with paper towels.

Mix the flour and 1/2 teaspoon salt in a bowl. Cut in the butter until crumbly. Add the cold water 1 tablespoon at a time, mixing well with a fork after each addition until the mixture forms a ball. Roll into an 11-inch circle on a lightly floured surface. Fit into a 10-inch pie plate, trimming and fluting the edge. Freeze for 30 minutes.

Spread the Dijon mustard over the pastry. Sprinkle with the basil. Layer the cheese and tomatoes over the basil. Beat the whipping cream, eggs and pepper in a mixing bowl until blended. Pour over the layers. Bake at 350 degrees for 30 minutes. Cool for 10 minutes before slicing.

Yield: 8 to 10 servings

Senator Bob Thompson's Secret Recipe for Home-Fried Potatoes

BOB THOMPSON, STATE SENATOR

1 medium white potato
¹/₄ Bermuda or Spanish onion
2 thick slices bacon
Worcestershire sauce to taste
Chesapeake Bay Seasoning to taste
Sea salt and freshly ground pepper to taste
Virgin olive oil

Cut the unpeeled potato and onion into slices. Cut the bacon into 1-inch pieces. Layer the potato, onion and bacon in a microwave-safe dish. Season with Worcestershire sauce, Bay Seasoning, sea salt and pepper to taste. Microwave, covered, for 15 minutes.

Heat olive oil in a large cast-iron skillet. Add the potato mixture. Cook until the potato is crisp and deep brown, turning occasionally. You may repeat this process for as many servings as you want. Serve with eggs and sausage or bacon.

Yield: 1 serving

Roasted Potatoes with Garlic and Herbs

12 small potatoes, or 6 medium potatoes
1/2 to 1 head garlic, or to taste
3 tablespoons olive oil
4 or 5 sprigs of rosemary, thyme or basil
    (each 4 to 6 inches long)

Scrub the unpeeled potatoes. Cut into 1/2-inch slices and pat dry. Separate the garlic into cloves and peel. Spread the olive oil in a 9×13-inch baking dish. Add the potatoes and garlic and toss to coat. Arrange in a single layer. Place the rosemary sprigs on top. Cover the baking dish with foil. Bake at 400 degrees for 20 minutes. Uncover and bake for 15 to 20 minutes longer or until the potatoes are tender and are just beginning to brown. Remove the rosemary sprigs and serve immediately.

Yield: 4 servings

EAST LYNN #1263 IS AN ACTIVE GRANGE IN
UNIONVILLE, EAST MARLBOROUGH TOWNSHIP.

Potatoes with Three Peppers

6 to 8 potatoes
3 tablespoons vegetable or corn oil
1/3 cup sliced scallions
1/2 teaspoon salt, or to taste
Freshly ground pepper to taste
1/3 cup chopped green bell pepper
1/3 cup chopped yellow bell pepper
1/3 cup chopped red bell pepper
1 tablespoon butter

Peel the potatoes. Cut into 1/2-inch cubes and place in a pan of cold water to keep from turning brown; drain. Fill a small saucepan with enough cold water to cover the potatoes. Bring to a boil and reduce the heat. Add the potatoes. Simmer for 1 to 2 minutes; drain.

Heat the oil in a skillet. Add the potatoes. Cook for 8 to 10 minutes or until the potatoes are golden brown, stirring and shaking the skillet as needed. Add the scallions, salt, pepper and bell peppers. Cook for 3 minutes, stirring gently. Add the butter. Cook for 2 minutes. Serve immediately. You may use 1/2 cup chopped green bell pepper and 1/2 cup chopped red bell pepper if yellow bell pepper is not available.

Yield: 6 to 8 servings

Scalloped Potatoes with Cheese

1 garlic clove, cut into halves
2¹/₂ pounds potatoes, peeled, cut into ¹/₈-inch slices
1¹/₂ cups grated Swiss cheese
6 tablespoons butter, cut into ¹/₄-inch pieces
1 teaspoon salt
¹/₈ teaspoon pepper
1¹/₄ cups milk

Rub the garlic over the surface of a 9×12-inch baking pan. Grease the pan. Layer the potatoes, Swiss cheese, butter, salt and pepper ¹/₂ at a time in the prepared pan. Pour the milk over the layers. Place on the top oven rack. Bake at 425 degrees for 20 minutes or until the potatoes are tender and brown on the top.

Yield: 8 servings

Cheddar Mashed Potatoes with Horseradish

2¹/₂ pounds russet potatoes
3 tablespoon butter, softened
4 ounces sharp Cheddar cheese, shredded
4 ounces white Cheddar cheese, shredded
¹/₂ cup (about) warm milk
2 tablespoons prepared horseradish
1 tablespoon chopped fresh chives or parsley
Salt and pepper to taste
1 tablespoon chopped fresh chives or parsley

Peel the potatoes and cut into 1¹/₂-inch pieces. Cook the potatoes in boiling water to cover in a saucepan for 18 minutes or until tender. Drain in a colander and return the potatoes to the saucepan. Mash the potatoes with a potato masher. Add the butter, sharp Cheddar cheese and white Cheddar cheese and mix until smooth. Add enough of the milk to make of the desired consistency and mix well. Stir in the horseradish and 1 tablespoon chives. Season with salt and pepper. Spoon into a serving bowl. Sprinkle with additional cheese and 1 tablespoon chives.

Yield: 8 servings

Three-Cheese Mashed Potatoes

2¹/₂ pounds Yukon Gold potatoes
3 tablespoons butter, softened
2¹/₂ cups mixed shredded cheese (such as
   smoked Gouda, Cheddar cheese and
   Swiss cheese)

¹/₂ cup (about) warm milk
4 slices bacon, crisp-cooked, crumbled
2 tablespoons chopped fresh sage, or
   2 teaspoons dried sage
Salt and pepper to taste

Peel the potatoes and cut into 1¹/₂-inch pieces. Cook the potatoes in boiling water to cover in a saucepan for 18 minutes or until tender. Drain in a colander and return the potatoes to the saucepan. Mash the potatoes with a potato masher. Stir in the butter and cheeses using a large kitchen fork. Add enough of the milk to make of the desired consistency. Stir in the bacon and sage. Season with salt and pepper.

Yield: 8 servings

Potato Dressing

3 cups chopped celery
2 cups chopped onion
1 small bunch parsley, finely chopped
   (1 cup)
2 tablespoons butter
5 pounds potatoes, peeled, chopped

¹/₂ cup (1 stick) butter, softened
Salt and pepper to taste
1 to 1¹/₂ cups milk
3 eggs, lightly beaten
1 cup saltine cracker crumbs
2 tablespoons butter, melted

Sauté the celery, onion and parsley in 2 tablespoons butter in a skillet until tender. Cook the potatoes in water to cover in a saucepan until tender; drain. Add ¹/₂ cup butter, salt and pepper and mix well. Add enough milk to make of the desired consistency, beating constantly. Stir in the eggs and cracker crumbs. Add the sautéed vegetables and mix well. Pour into a buttered 9×13-inch baking dish. Drizzle with 2 tablespoons butter. Bake at 350 degrees for 30 minutes or until light brown on top. Serve with turkey or chicken.

Yield: 12 servings

Marbled Potatoes

1 pound sweet potatoes, cooked, peeled
1 pound red or white potatoes, cooked, peeled
2 large scallions, chopped
1/4 cup (1/2 stick) butter or margarine
1/2 cup sour cream or plain yogurt
1/2 cup whipping cream, whipped

1 teaspoon salt
1/2 teaspoon pepper
Nutmeg to taste
1/4 cup fresh bread crumbs
2 tablespoons butter or margarine, melted
2 tablespoons minced fresh parsley

Mash the sweet potatoes and red potatoes in separate bowls. Sauté the scallions in 1/4 cup butter in a skillet until tender. Stir 1/2 of the scallions into each bowl of potatoes. Whisk the sour cream with the whipped cream in a bowl. Fold 1/2 of the sour cream mixture into each potato mixture. Add 1/2 of the salt, pepper and nutmeg to each bowl. Layer the sweet potato mixture and red potato mixture 1/2 at a time in a greased 1-quart soufflé dish. Swirl with a knife to marbleize. Sprinkle with a mixture of the bread crumbs, 2 tablespoons butter and parsley. Bake at 350 degrees for 30 to 35 minutes or until the topping is golden brown. You may freeze this dish before baking if desired.

Yield: 6 servings

Sweet Potato Casserole

3 cups mashed cooked sweet potatoes
1 cup sugar
1/2 cup (1 stick) butter, melted
2 eggs, beaten
1 teaspoon vanilla extract

1/3 cup milk
1/2 cup packed brown sugar
1/4 cup flour
2 1/2 tablespoons butter, melted
1/2 cup chopped pecans

Combine the sweet potatoes, sugar, butter, eggs, vanilla and milk in a bowl and beat until smooth. Spoon into a 2-quart baking dish. Mix the brown sugar, flour, 2 1/2 tablespoons butter and pecans in a small bowl. Spread over the sweet potato mixture. Bake at 350 degrees until cooked through and the top is golden brown.

Yield: 6 to 8 servings

Marinated Herb Vegetables

2 cups sliced zucchini
1 1/2 cups chopped red bell pepper
1 1/2 cups sliced yellow squash
2 cups chopped cauliflower
1 1/2 cups snap green bean pieces
1 large red onion, sliced
1 cup sliced carrot
1/4 cup balsamic vinegar
2 tablespoons olive oil
3/4 teaspoon basil
3/4 teaspoon tarragon
1/2 teaspoon oregano
1/2 teaspoon thyme
1/2 teaspoon parsley
1/2 teaspoon rosemary
1/4 teaspoon pepper
4 garlic cloves, crushed

Combine the zucchini, bell peppers, squash, cauliflower, green beans, onion and carrot in a large bowl. Mix the balsamic vinegar, olive oil, basil, tarragon, oregano, thyme, parsley, rosemary, pepper and garlic in a bowl. Pour over the vegetables and toss to coat well. Place in a 9×13-inch baking dish. Bake, covered, at 425 degrees for 40 minutes or until the vegetables are tender. You may also serve over hot cooked pasta or rice.

Yield: 10 servings

Microwave Stir-Fried Vegetables

1 tablespoon vegetable oil
1 tablespoon butter
3 medium onions, cut into quarters
1 medium green bell pepper, cut into strips $1/4$ inch wide
3 cups thinly sliced cabbage
3 medium carrots, diagonally sliced
1 cup broccoli florets
1 cup cauliflower florets
3 ribs celery, diagonally sliced
$1/4$ cup sliced green onions
1 (10-ounce) package frozen pea pods
$1/4$ cup water
$1/4$ cup soy sauce
2 teaspoons cornstarch
1 teaspoon sugar

Place the vegetable oil, butter and onions in a 5-quart microwave-safe dish. Microwave, uncovered, on High for 3 minutes or until hot. Add the bell pepper, cabbage, carrots, broccoli, cauliflower, celery, green onions and pea pods and mix well. Microwave, covered, on High for 4 minutes.

Mix the water, soy sauce, cornstarch and sugar in a bowl. Add to the vegetables and toss gently to coat. Microwave, uncovered, on High for 4 to 6 minutes or until heated through. Serve over hot cooked rice or Chinese noodles. You may add 4 cups thinly sliced cooked chicken if desired.

Yield: 6 to 8 servings

(MICROWAVE GUIDELINES, continued)

*When preparing sauces and gravies in the microwave, remove from the microwave and stir briskly when the edges begin to thicken to prevent lumps from forming.
*Microwave pierced potatoes upright in microwave-safe muffin cups for baked potatoes with dry skin.
*Microwave nuts on High for 2 minutes because they are easier to chop while warm.
*Microwave garlic cloves on High for 10 to 20 seconds to make them easier to peel.

Chocolate Zucchini Spice Cake

2¹/2 cups flour
¹/2 cup baking cocoa
2¹/2 teaspoons baking powder
1¹/2 teaspoons baking soda
1 teaspoon salt
³/4 cup (1¹/2 sticks) margarine, softened
2 cups sugar

3 eggs
¹/2 cup milk
2 teaspoons vanilla extract
2 teaspoons cinnamon
³/4 teaspoon nutmeg
2 cups grated zucchini
Cream Cheese Frosting

Mix the flour, baking cocoa, baking powder, baking soda and salt together. Cream the margarine and sugar in a mixing bowl until light and fluffy. Add the eggs 1 at a time, beating well after each addition. Add the flour mixture and milk alternately, beating well after each addition. Stir in the vanilla, cinnamon and nutmeg. Fold in the zucchini. Pour into 2 greased and floured 9-inch round cake pans. Bake at 350 degrees for 30 minutes or until the cake tests done. Cool in the pans for 5 minutes. Remove to wire racks to cool completely. Spread Cream Cheese Frosting between the layers and over the top and side of the cake.

Yield: 12 servings

Cream Cheese Frosting

3 ounces cream cheese, softened
¹/3 cup margarine, softened
³/4 teaspoon cinnamon

4 cups confectioners' sugar
1 teaspoon vanilla extract
1¹/2 to 2 tablespoons milk or water

Beat the cream cheese, margarine and cinnamon in a mixing bowl until fluffy. Add the confectioners' sugar. Beat at low speed until combined. Add the vanilla and milk. Beat at high speed for 2 minutes.

Yield: 5 cups frosting

Grandma's Pumpkin Pie

1/2 cup sugar
1/4 cup packed brown sugar
1 teaspoon flour
1 1/2 cups cooked pumpkin
3 eggs, beaten

1 cup milk
2 teaspoons pumpkin pie spice
1 tablespoon butter
1 unbaked (9-inch) pie shell
Cinnamon to taste

Mix the sugar, brown sugar and flour in a small bowl. Combine the sugar mixture and pumpkin in a mixing bowl and mix well. Add the eggs, milk and pumpkin pie spice and mix well. Heat the butter in a skillet until melted and brown. Stir into the pumpkin mixture. Pour into the pie shell. Sprinkle with cinnamon. Bake at 400 degrees for 15 minutes. Reduce the oven temperature to 350 degrees. Bake for 40 to 45 minutes or until a knife inserted in the center comes out clean.

Yield: 8 servings

Butternut Squash Pie

THIS IS A SPECIAL RECIPE FROM MARY S. KIRK. HER GRANDDAUGHTER NOW ENJOYS MAKING IT.

2 cups mashed cooked butternut squash
1 cup evaporated milk
3 eggs, lightly beaten
1/2 cup packed brown sugar
1/2 cup sugar
2 tablespoons flour
1/2 teaspoon lemon extract

1/2 teaspoon cinnamon
1/4 teaspoon nutmeg
1/4 teaspoon cloves
1/8 teaspoon salt
1 teaspoon butter, melted
1 unbaked (9-inch) pie shell, chilled

Combine the squash, evaporated milk, eggs, brown sugar and sugar in a mixing bowl and mix well. Add the flour, lemon extract, cinnamon, nutmeg, cloves, salt and butter. Beat at medium speed for 5 minutes. Pour into the pie shell. Cover the edge of the pie shell with foil to prevent overbrowning. Bake at 400 degrees for 10 minutes. Reduce the oven temperature to 375 degrees. Bake for 25 minutes. Remove the foil. Bake for 10 to 15 minutes longer or until a knife inserted in the center comes out clean and the crust is golden brown.

Yield: 8 servings

Pesto

3 cups fresh basil leaves
4 garlic cloves
$^1/_4$ teaspoon salt
$^3/_4$ cup freshly grated Parmesan cheese
$^1/_4$ cup finely ground pine nuts or walnuts
$^1/_2$ cup olive oil

Process the basil, garlic, salt, Parmesan cheese, pine nuts and olive oil in a food processor until a thick paste forms. Use to toss with hot cooked pasta or to perk up any pasta dish. You may make extra and freeze in small quantities in sealable freezer bags.

Yield: $2^1/_2$ cups pesto

Canned Salsa

16 large tomatoes, peeled, chopped
2 green bell peppers, chopped
10 hot peppers, chopped
2 onions, chopped
3 garlic cloves, chopped
1 cup cider vinegar
1 (12-ounce) can tomato paste
Seasoned salt to taste

Combine the tomatoes, bell peppers, hot peppers, onions, garlic, cider vinegar, tomato paste and seasoned salt in a large saucepan. Bring to a boil and reduce the heat. Simmer for 10 minutes. Ladle into hot sterilized 1-pint jars, leaving $^1/_2$ inch headspace; seal with 2-piece lids. Process in a boiling water bath for 30 minutes.

Yield: about 6 pints salsa

Fruit AND *Wine*

SPONSOR: PRODUCE FOR BETTER HEALTH FOUNDATION

The apple harvest has arrived at Glen Willow Orchards, Avondale.

The Produce for Better Health Foundation is the catalyst for creating a healthier America through increased consumption of fruits and vegetables. The Foundation is a nonprofit organization which, in cooperation with the National Cancer Institute, sponsors the national 5 A Day—for Better Health Program. Together with health and government agencies and the fruit and vegetable industry, the program teaches that eating five or more daily servings of fruit and vegetables reduces risk of illness.

Produce for Better Health Foundation
5301 Limestone Road, Suite 101
Wilmington, Delaware 19808-1249
Phone: 302-235-2329
Fax: 302-235-5555
www.5aday.com

VINEYARDS TAKE ADVANTAGE OF CHESTER COUNTY'S
EXCELLENT CLIMATE. APPLES ARE PLENTIFUL EACH AUTUMN.

McIntosh Apple and Bleu Cheese Bisque

1 tablespoon unsalted butter
2 McIntosh apples, peeled, cored, coarsely chopped
1 1/2 cups milk
5 to 6 ounces bleu cheese
Salt and pepper to taste

Melt the butter in a 2-quart saucepan over medium heat. Add the apples. Sauté until the apples are soft. Add the milk and reduce the heat. Add the cheese a small amount at a time when the milk begins to be scalded around the edge, stirring constantly. The milk may begin to separate, but just keep adding the cheese, stirring constantly. Season with salt and pepper to taste.

Yield: 2 servings

Chilled Creamy Peach Soup

6 medium fresh peaches, peeled, sliced
3 tablespoons lemon juice
1/2 cup sugar
1 teaspoon almond extract
2 cups half-and-half or heavy cream
1/2 cup slivered almonds

Process the peaches, lemon juice, sugar and almond extract in a blender until smooth. Add the half-and-half. Process at low speed until blended. Pour into a bowl. Chill, covered, in the refrigerator until serving time.

Place the almonds on a baking sheet. Bake at 325 degrees for 8 to 12 minutes or until toasted, stirring once or twice. Ladle the chilled soup into serving bowls. Garnish with the toasted almonds.

Yield: 6 servings

Apple Salad

1 egg
1 tablespoon flour
$^1/_2$ cup water
$^1/_2$ cup sugar
1 tablespoon butter
1 tablespoon vinegar
$^1/_8$ teaspoon salt

4 apples, cored, chopped
2 bananas, sliced
$^1/_2$ cup raisins
1 cup chopped celery
$^1/_2$ cup chopped nuts
1 cup miniature
   marshmallows

Combine the egg, flour, water, sugar, butter, vinegar and salt in a saucepan. Bring to a boil. Cook until thickened and smooth, stirring constantly. Remove from the heat and let cool. Combine the apples, bananas, raisins, celery, nuts and marshmallows in a bowl and toss to mix. Add the cooled dressing and toss to coat.

Yield: 4 to 6 servings

Cranberry Orange Salad

1 (3-ounce) package
   strawberry or cherry gelatin
1 cup boiling water
$^1/_2$ cup cold water
2 cups fresh cranberries

1 orange, seeded, cut into
   quarters
2 apples, seeded, cut into
   quarters
3 tablespoons sugar

Dissolve the gelatin in the boiling water in a heatproof bowl. Stir in the cold water. Chill until thickened. Process the cranberries, orange and apples in a food processor until coarsely chopped. Stir in the sugar. Let stand for a few minutes. Fold into the thickened gelatin. Spoon into salad molds. Chill until firm. Unmold onto salad plates and garnish as desired.

Yield: 4 servings

Nutty Apple Salad

Process 3 tablespoons peanut butter, 2 tablespoons mayonnaise and 1 tablespoon sugar in a food processor until smooth. Core and cut 4 or 5 apples into pieces. Combine the apples, $^1/_2$ cup walnuts or peanuts and $^1/_2$ cup raisins in a bowl. Add the peanut butter mixture and toss to coat. Serve immediately.

Yield: 4 to 6 servings

Strawberry Pretzel Salad

2 cups thin pretzel sticks, crushed
3/4 cup (1 1/2 sticks) margarine, melted
2 teaspoons sugar
1 (6-ounce) package strawberry gelatin
2 cups boiling water
2 (10-ounce) packages frozen strawberries, partially thawed
8 ounces cream cheese, softened
1 cup sugar
9 ounces whipped topping

Mix the pretzel crumbs, margarine and 2 teaspoons sugar in a bowl. Press into a 9×13-inch glass baking dish. Bake at 375 degrees for 8 minutes. Let stand until cool. Dissolve the gelatin in the boiling water in a medium heatproof bowl. Stir in the strawberries. Place in the freezer and freeze until partially set, stirring frequently. Beat the cream cheese and 1 cup sugar in a mixing bowl until smooth. Fold in the whipped topping. Spread over the cooled pretzel layer. Top with the strawberry mixture. Chill until set.

Yield: 12 servings

Strawberry Nut Salad

1 (6-ounce) package strawberry gelatin
1 cup boiling water
2 (10-ounce) packages frozen strawberries, thawed
1 (20-ounce) can crushed pineapple, drained
3 medium ripe bananas, mashed
1 cup coarsely chopped pecans
2 cups sour cream

Dissolve the gelatin in the boiling water in a heatproof bowl. Fold in the undrained strawberries, drained pineapple, bananas and pecans. Place 1/2 of the strawberry mixture in a salad mold. Chill until set. Spread with the sour cream. Top with the remaining strawberry mixture. Chill until firm. Unmold onto a serving plate. Garnish with a dollop of additional sour cream.

Yield: 6 to 8 servings

Strawberry Pecan Bread

3 cups flour
2 cups sugar
2 teaspoons baking soda
1 teaspoon salt
1 tablespoon cinnamon
4 eggs, beaten
2 1/4 cups vegetable oil
2 cups chopped strawberries
1 1/4 cups chopped pecans

Mix the flour, sugar, baking soda, salt and cinnamon in a bowl. Add the eggs, vegetable oil, strawberries and pecans and mix until moistened. Spoon into 2 greased 5x9-inch loaf pans. Bake at 350 degrees for 55 minutes or until the loaves test done. Cool in the pans for 5 minutes. Remove to wire racks to cool completely.

Yield: 2 loaves

Apple Crisp

5 cups sliced peeled apples
2 to 4 tablespoons sugar
1/2 cup rolled oats
1/2 cup packed brown sugar
1/4 cup flour
1/4 teaspoon nutmeg, ginger or cinnamon
1/4 cup (1/2 stick) butter or margarine

Combine the apples and sugar in a bowl and toss to coat. Place in an 8-inch round baking dish. Mix the oats, brown sugar, flour and nutmeg in a bowl. Cut in the butter until crumbly. Sprinkle over the apples. Bake at 375 degrees for 30 to 35 minutes or until the apples are tender and the topping is golden brown.

Yield: 4 to 6 servings

German Kuchen

1/2 cup (1 stick) butter, softened
1 egg
1 cup flour
1 teaspoon baking powder
1/8 teaspoon salt
1/2 cup (about) sugar
1/4 to 1/3 cup milk

3 or 4 apples, peaches or small ripe
   Italian plums grown in Chester
   County
Cinnamon-sugar to taste
1/4 to 1/2 cup flour
2 to 3 tablespoons sugar
1/4 cup (1/2 stick) margarine

Combine 1/2 cup butter, egg, 1 cup flour, baking powder, salt, about 1/2 cup sugar and milk in a bowl and mix to form a soft dough. Place in a greased and lightly floured 8-inch round baking pan. Press the dough over the bottom and up the side of the pan. Peel the apples and cut into slices. Layer the apples over the dough. Sprinkle with cinnamon-sugar. Mix 1/4 to 1/2 cup flour and 2 to 3 tablespoons sugar in a bowl. Cut in 1/4 cup margarine until crumbly. Sprinkle over the apples. Bake at 350 degrees for 30 minutes. Cool for 10 minutes. Remove carefully from the pan to a wire rack to cool completely. Serve warm or cold with whipped cream or ice cream.

Yield: 6 to 8 servings

FRESH FRUITS AND VEGETABLES ABOUND AT
YEAGERS FARM MARKET ON KIMBERTON ROAD,
ROUTE #113, IN EAST PIKELAND TOWNSHIP.

Rhubarb Crunch

> 6 cups chopped rhubarb
> 1 1/2 cups sugar
> 1/4 cup flour
> 1/2 cup packed brown sugar
> 1/2 cup rolled oats
> 1/2 cup (1 stick) butter
> 3/4 cup flour

Combine the rhubarb, sugar and 1/4 cup flour in a bowl and mix well. Place in a greased 9×13-inch baking dish. Mix the brown sugar, oats, butter and 3/4 cup flour in a bowl until crumbly. Place over the rhubarb mixture. Bake at 375 degrees for 40 minutes. Serve topped with your favorite ice cream.

> Yield: 12 servings

Rhubarb and Cream

> 4 cups 1-inch pieces rhubarb
> 1 cup water
> 1 1/2 to 2 cups sugar or packed brown sugar
> 3 to 4 tablespoons Minute tapioca

Combine the rhubarb, water, 1 cup of the sugar and tapioca in a saucepan. Cook, partially covered, over low heat until the rhubarb begins to disintegrate, stirring occasionally. Add 1/2 cup of the remaining sugar and mix well. Adjust to taste with the remaining sugar. Cook for 5 minutes. Pour into a large bowl. Chill, covered, in the refrigerator until thickened. Serve with heavy cream.

> Yield: 8 servings

Pineapple Delight

3 medium eggs
3 tablespoons flour
1/2 cup pineapple juice
1 cup sugar-free whipped
  topping
1 (20-ounce) can pineapple
  chunks, partially drained

2 oranges, cut into
  sections, seeded
2 bananas, sliced
1/2 cup pecan pieces
  (optional)

Combine the eggs, flour and pineapple juice in a saucepan and mix well. Cook until thickened, stirring constantly. Remove from the heat and cool. Fold in the whipped topping. Combine the pineapple, oranges, bananas and pecans in a large bowl. Add the cooled mixture and toss to mix well.

Yield: 10 to 12 servings

Peaches and Cream Trifle

1 (3-ounce) package instant
  vanilla pudding mix
1 3/4 cups milk
12 ounces whipped topping
7 peaches, peeled, sliced

3 tablespoons sugar
1 (16-ounce) loaf frozen
  pound cake
1/2 cup orange juice
1/4 cup almonds, toasted

Mix the instant pudding mix and milk in a bowl until thickened. Fold in 1/2 of the whipped topping. Toss the peaches with sugar in a bowl. Cut enough of the pound cake into cubes to measure 6 cups. Place 1/2 of the cake cubes in a 3-quart trifle bowl. Sprinkle with 1/2 of the orange juice. Layer 1/2 of the pudding mixture and 1/2 of the peaches over the cake. Repeat the layers with the remaining cake, orange juice, pudding mixture and peaches. Spread the remaining whipped topping over the top. Chill, covered, for 8 hours. Sprinkle with the almonds before serving.

Yield: 14 servings

PEACH COOLER

Process 1/2 cup chilled coarsely chopped peaches, 3/4 cup chilled milk, 1/4 teaspoon sugar and 2 or 3 drops of almond extract in a blender until smooth. Add 1/2 cup ice cream. Process at the Stir Setting for 3 to 5 seconds. Pour into tall glasses to serve.

Yield: 1 1/2 cups

Frozen Strawberry Soufflé

2 (10-ounce) packages frozen sliced
   strawberries, thawed
6 egg yolks
3/4 cup sugar
1/2 cup orange liqueur
1 cup sugar
1/3 cup fresh orange juice

6 egg whites
3 cups whipping cream, whipped
Few drops of red food coloring
   (optional)
1 cup chopped walnuts
Whipped cream
Fresh whole strawberries

Cut a piece of waxed paper to form a collar in a 2-quart soufflé dish, extending 2 to 3 inches above the rim. Grease the dish and waxed paper. Purée the thawed sliced strawberries in a blender or food processor.

Beat the egg yolks and 3/4 cup sugar in a mixing bowl until thick and pale yellow. Stir in 1/2 of the strawberry purée. Pour into a double boiler. Cook over simmering water for 15 minutes or until the mixture thickens and coats a spoon, stirring constantly. Remove from the heat. Let stand until cool. Stir in the orange liqueur.

Combine 1 cup sugar and orange juice in a saucepan. Heat until the sugar dissolves, stirring constantly. Cook to 232 to 234 degrees on a candy thermometer, spun-thread stage; do not stir.

Beat the egg whites in a mixing bowl until stiff peaks form. Add the hot orange syrup in a fine stream, beating constantly at high speed. Let stand until cool. Fold the whipped cream and remaining strawberry purée into the cooled strawberry mixture. Fold in the orange meringue. Stir in the food coloring. Spoon into the prepared soufflé dish. Freeze for 6 to 12 hours.

To serve, remove the collar and press the walnuts into the side of the soufflé. Decorate the top with dollops of additional whipped cream. Mound whole strawberries in the center.

   Yield: 12 servings

Irene Webb's Apple Cake

THE WEBB FAMILY HAS BEEN PART OF CHESTER COUNTY FOR OVER 300
YEARS. THIS RECIPE IS UNDOUBTEDLY NEWER THAN THAT, BUT IT WAS A
FAVORITE AT WEBB REUNIONS AS LONG AS IRENE WAS ALIVE.

$1^2/_3$ cups sifted flour
1 teaspoon cinnamon
1 teaspoon nutmeg
$^1/_4$ teaspoon cloves
1 teaspoon baking soda
$^1/_2$ cup cold coffee
$^1/_2$ cup (1 stick) butter, softened
1 cup sugar
1 egg
1 cup raisins
1 cup chopped apple
$^1/_2$ cup coarsely chopped nuts

Grease an 8×8-inch cake pan. Line the bottom with waxed paper. Sift the sifted flour, cinnamon, nutmeg and cloves together. Dissolve the baking soda in the coffee.

Cream the butter and sugar in a mixing bowl until light. Add the egg and beat until fluffy. Add the coffee mixture alternately with the flour mixture, beating constantly. Stir in the raisins, apple and nuts. Pour into the prepared cake pan. Bake at 350 degrees for 45 minutes or until the cake tests done. Serve plain, frosted or with vanilla ice cream. This cake freezes well.

Yield: 9 servings

Pineapple Cake

TIM HENNESSEY, STATE REPRESENTATIVE

2 cups flour
2 cups sugar
2 eggs
2 teaspoons baking soda
1 (20-ounce) can crushed pineapple

8 ounces cream cheese, softened
$1/2$ cup (1 stick) butter, softened
$1^1/2$ cups confectioners' sugar
Coarsely chopped walnuts

Combine the flour, sugar, eggs, baking soda and undrained pineapple in a large bowl and mix well with a spoon. Pour into a greased 9×13-inch cake pan. Bake at 350 degrees for 35 to 45 minutes or until the cake tests done. Cool in the pan on a wire rack.

Beat the cream cheese, butter and confectioners' sugar in a mixing bowl until smooth and creamy. Spread over the cooled cake. Sprinkle with walnuts.

Yield: 15 servings

Creamy Apple Pie

TIM HENNESSEY, STATE REPRESENTATIVE

8 ounces cream cheese, softened
$1/4$ cup sugar
1 egg
$1/2$ teaspoon vanilla extract

1 unbaked (10-inch) pie shell
5 to 7 Granny Smith apples
$2/3$ cup sugar
$1/2$ teaspoon cinnamon

Beat the cream cheese, $1/4$ cup sugar, egg and vanilla in a mixing bowl until smooth. Spread in the pie shell. Core and peel the apples. Cut into slices and place in a bowl. Add $2/3$ cup sugar and cinnamon and toss to coat. Arrange over the cream cheese mixture. Bake at 400 degrees for 15 minutes. Reduce the oven temperature to 350 degrees. Bake for 30 to 40 minutes longer. Serve with ice cream or whipped cream.

Yield: 8 servings

Better Cheddar Apple Pie

1 cup sugar
2 tablespoons flour
1 teaspoon cinnamon
1 teaspoon grated lemon zest
1/8 teaspoon cloves, ground
Salt to taste
6 tart New York cooking apples, peeled, thinly sliced
1 unbaked (9-inch) pie shell
1/2 cup flour
1/4 cup sugar
1 cup shredded Wisconsin sharp Cheddar cheese
1/4 cup (1/2 stick) margarine, melted
Sour cream

Mix 1 cup sugar, 2 tablespoons flour, cinnamon, lemon zest, cloves and salt in a bowl. Add the apples and toss to coat. Arrange in the pie shell. Combine 1/2 cup flour, 1/4 cup sugar and cheese in a bowl and mix well. Add the margarine and mix until crumbly. Sprinkle over the apples. Bake at 400 degrees for 40 minutes or until the topping and crust are golden brown. Serve with sour cream.

Yield: 8 servings

APPLE A DAY

"An apple a day keeps the doctor away." We have all heard this saying, and now there is scientific evidence it is really a fact.

Food scientists at Cornell University have found that it is the phytochemicals in the flesh of the apple but even more so in the skin, that provides the fruit's antioxidant and anti-cancer benefits.

So there you have it. Eat your apples or call the doctor. Which will it be?

Fresh Blueberry Pie

1 cup sugar
3 tablespoons cornstarch
1/4 teaspoon salt
3 tablespoons black cherry gelatin
1 cup boiling water
1 quart fresh blueberries
1 baked (9-inch) pie shell

Mix the sugar, cornstarch, salt and gelatin in a heatproof bowl. Add the boiling water and stir until dissolved. Let stand until cool. Arrange the blueberries in the pie shell. Pour the cooled mixture over the blueberries. Chill, covered, in the refrigerator until set. Serve with whipped cream, whipped topping or ice cream.

Yield: 8 servings

Blueberry Sour Cream Pie

CAROLE RUBLEY, STATE REPRESENTATIVE

1 pint fresh blueberries
1/2 cup packed light brown sugar
2 cups sour cream
1 egg, beaten
3 tablespoons flour
3 tablespoons light brown sugar
1 unbaked (9-inch) pie shell

Toss the blueberries and 1/2 cup brown sugar in a bowl. Mix the sour cream, egg, flour and 3 tablespoons brown sugar in a large bowl. Fold in the blueberry mixture. Spoon into the pie shell. Bake at 425 degrees for 35 to 40 minutes or until a knife inserted in the center comes out clean.

Yield: 8 servings

BERRY SAUCE

Raspberries, blackberries and wine berries are a few of the berries growing wild on the edge of country roads and woodlands in Chester County. You can just eat them as you find them, but they can be enjoyed a bit longer by preparing this delicious sauce.

Cook 1 quart berries and 1 cup sugar in a saucepan until slightly thickened, stirring constantly. Serve the sauce with ice cream or pancakes. You may also place the berries and sugar in a microwave-safe bowl and microwave on High for 3 minutes, stirring twice.

Peaches and Cream Pie

3 to 5 peaches, peeled, cut into halves
1 unbaked (9-inch) pie shell
2/3 cup sugar
1/4 cup flour
1/4 teaspoon salt
1/2 teaspoon cinnamon
1 cup whipping cream

Place the peach halves cut side down in the pie shell. Combine the sugar, flour, salt, cinnamon and whipping cream in a medium mixing bowl and beat well using a whisk. Pour over the peach halves. Bake at 400 degrees for 35 to 40 minutes or until the pie tests done. Cool before serving.

Yield: 8 servings

Delicious Strawberry Pie

3/4 cup sugar
1 (3-ounce) package strawberry gelatin
3 tablespoons cornstarch
1 cup boiling water
1 quart strawberries, rinsed, hulled
1 baked (9-inch) pie shell
Whipped cream or whipped topping

Combine the sugar, gelatin, cornstarch and boiling water in a saucepan. Boil for 1 minute. Place the strawberries in the pie shell. Pour the gelatin mixture over the strawberries. Chill in the refrigerator until firm. Serve with whipped cream or whipped topping.

Yield: 8 servings

The Vineyards and Wineries of Chester County

ERIC MILLER, CHADDSFORD WINEMAKER AND PROPRIETOR

It has become a common and welcome sight for visitors to Chester County to see winery and tasting room signs along the highways and back roads. There are currently five wineries in Chester County, the largest and most recognized of which is the Chaddsford Winery in the rural village of Chadds Ford. Led by Chaddsford Winery, the region's wines have received national recognition and glowing reviews in publications like *USA Today*, *Bon Appétit*, and *Wine Spectator*. No wonder that both locals and out-of-towners take to the countryside on weekends for the relaxing summer concerts, wine festivals, opportunities to picnic with family and friends, tours of the winemaking and barrel-aging cellars, and—of course—tastings of the current vintage!

At the end of the twentieth century, significant new vineyard acreage has also been planted in Chester County, using the latest clones of traditional world-class varieties like Cabernet Sauvignon, Merlot, Pinot Noir, and Chardonnay. These progressive vineyards represent large agricultural investments incorporating the latest technology and are geared to produce maximum quality grapes that will put Chester County on the "wine map" with other respected wine regions like California, France, and Italy. Stay tuned for continuing growth of this exciting "farm" industry in Chester County!

CHESTER COUNTY'S BEST-KNOWN WINES: Dry White: Chardonnay, Pinot Grigio; Dry Red: Cabernet Franc, Pinot Noir, Chambourcin; Sweeter Wines: Blush, Riesling, Niagara

MATURE GRAPEVINES GREET THE VISITOR AT CHADDSFORD WINERY ON BALTIMORE PIKE, ROUTE #1. THE WINERY PROVIDES A PLEASANT SETTING FOR THE WINE CONNOISSEUR.

Wine Punches and Mulled Wines

Almost any wine can be used to add flavor and moisture to your favorite recipes (not to mention a little fun to your cooking experience). Don't worry about how much, what kind, whether the wine is expensive or inexpensive, whether the bottle is just opened or "leftover" from another great meal. Just go with what is called the Barbara Walters approach—take the bottle and pour it over whatever you're cooking and be assured that it will taste even better for the effort! In addition to using wine in all your favorite recipes, use it to liven up your holiday entertainment, your outdoor summer parties, and just about any occasion year-round by making wine punches and hot mulled wines. Here are a few favorites to get you started.

Chaddsford Niagara Limosa

1 bottle Chaddsford Niagara
1 (12-ounce) can lemonade concentrate
1/2 cup sugar
3 cups club soda

Mix the wine, lemonade concentrate and sugar in a pitcher. Stir in the club soda gradually. Chill in the refrigerator. Pour into a punch bowl. Garnish with sliced strawberries and limes. You may add a frozen ice ring with flowers if desired.

Yield: 8 servings

Chaddsford Tropical Sangria

3 cups pineapple juice drink
1/4 cup sugar
Broken whole cinnamon sticks to taste
Ground nutmeg to taste
1 bottle Chaddsford Proprietors Reserve White
3 cups ginger ale

Mix the pineapple drink, sugar, cinnamon sticks and nutmeg in a pitcher. Chill, covered, for 8 to 12 hours. Pour the pineapple mixture in a punch bowl just before serving. Add the wine and ginger ale. Add ice. Garnish with orange slices.

Yield: 8 servings

Slow-Cooker Cranberry Apple Wine

1 bottle Chaddsford Spiced Apple Wine
2 cups cranberry juice
$^1/_2$ cup sugar
1 orange

Whole cloves
Whole cinnamon sticks
Apple slices

Pour the wine and cranberry juice into a slow cooker. Stir in the sugar. Cook on Low until heated through. Stud the orange with cloves. Place the studded orange and cinnamon sticks in the wine mixture. Add apple slices. Serve warm.

Yield: 5 servings

Chaddsford Harvest Grog

1 quart apple cider
2 bottles Chaddsford Spiced Apple Wine
3 tablespoons honey
2 tablespoons sugar
$^1/_8$ teaspoon cinnamon

$^1/_8$ teaspoon nutmeg
Whole cinnamon sticks
1 apple
Whole cloves

Combine the apple cider, wine, honey, sugar, cinnamon and nutmeg in a slow cooker. Cook on Low until heated through. Add the cinnamon sticks. Stud the apple with whole cloves. Float in the wine mixture.

Yield: 10 servings

Grand Holiday Spirit

2 bottles Chaddsford Holiday Spirit Wine
5 cups orange juice

1 cup Grand Marnier
$^1/_2$ cup honey or sugar

Combine the wine, orange juice, liqueur and honey in a slow cooker. Cook on Low until heated through. Serve warm.

Yield: 12 servings

Gift

When God had finished with his plan,

He paused his handiwork to scan—

There the world in splendor stood,

Hill and river, field and wood,

Mountain range and shining seas,

Fern and flower, valley, trees;

Rock and meadow sown with clover,

Sun and moon and cloud set over;

Prairie, island, lake and bay

All complete on that sixth day.

"I think," He mused, "I'll give a bounty—"

And that's how we got Chester County.

Edward Shenton

BIBLIOGRAPHY

Davidson, Jane L. S. "Roger Hunt Mill." National Register of Historic Places nomination, 1979.

Futhey, J. Smith, and Cope, Gilbert. *History of Chester County, Pennsylvania*. Philadelphia: Louis H. Everts, 1881.

Powell, Doris. *Spring Mill, 1793*. Frazer: East Whiteland Township, nd.

The Mill at Anselma. Pottstown: The French and Pickering Creeks Conservation Trust, Inc., nd.

Washington, D.C. National Archives. Microcopy Collection, M247. "Papers of the Continental Congress."

Washington, D.C. National Archives. Microcopy Collection. "Tenth Census of the United States. Agricultural Production."

West Chester. Chester County Historical Society. Clippings Collection.

West Whiteland Township Historical Commission. *Thomas Mill and Miller's House*. Pennsylvania Historic Resource Survey Form, 1983.

Recipe Contributors

American Mushroom Institute
Lori Baer
Patricia Baldwin
Brenda Beitler
Pat Boston
Dorothy Brosius
Mary Buffington
Jane Buffum
Buona Foods, Inc.
Jennifer Carl
Lynne Carroll
Cattlemen's Beef Association
Chaddsford Winery
Tina Coccie
Betty Collins
Jane Collins
Country Fresh Mushroom Company
Sarah Darlington
Christina Davidson
Jane Davidson
Lydia McCoury Davidson
Sarah Davis
Devault Foods
Andrew Dinniman, *Commissioner*
Sheila Dusinberre
Cheryl Eckman
Phyllis Ferguson
Sarah Finnaren
David Fisher
Bob Flick, *Representative*
Dottie Freese
Jim Gerlach, *Senator*
Sally Gregor
Mary Gyger
Colin Hanna, *Commissioner*
Samuel Hayes, *PA Secretary of Agriculture*
Tim Hennessey, *Representative*
Art Hershey, *Representative*

Clair Hershey
Joyce Hershey
Marilyn Hershey
Linda Hemphill Hicks
Barbara Hill
Peg Hindman
Diana Hoopes
Maureen Horesh
Betsy Huber
Judy Ishler
Kathy Kaiser
Erma Kauffman
Barbara Kelly
Dorothy Kimball
Hannah Kirk
Mary Kirk
Stella Kirk
Eleanor Krapf
Dawn Kulp
Edie Kurtz
Sue Lamborn
Marilyn McComsey Latham
Kathy Linough
Joy Losey
Karen Martynick, *Commissioner*
Melba Mathews
Deb McCaffrey
Tom McCaffrey
June McMichael
Bob McRae
Eric Miller
Margaret S. Miller
Susan Miller
Carol Miner
Nancy Mohr
Sally Moore
Paul O'Toole, *Executive Chef*
Pennsylvania Pork Producers
Ada Philips
Phillips Mushroom Company

Keith Pindzak
Lois Porter
June Pratt
Charlene Ranck
Marilyn Raub
Peggy Ray
Clair Rennie
Marie Riehl
Janet Robinson
Chris Ross, *Representative*
Carole Rubley, *Representative*
Judy Schell
Gerald Schreck, *Executive Chef*
Curt Schroder, *Representative*
Linda Schweikert
Dolores Semasek
Hazel Sensenig
Beth Slack
Darlene Snyder
Erich Snyder
Hannah Snyder
Mary Sproat
Benuel Stoltzfus
Melvin Stoltzfus
Samuel Stoltzfus
Nancy Swarr
Elinor Z. Taylor, *Representative*
Robert Thompson, *Senator*
Donna Tomanelli
Raquel Trice
Karen Vollmecke
Sandy Wagner
Lynore Walsleben
Charles Warren
Renee Washington
Ruth Whittaker
Betsy Wilkinson
Carolyn Williams
Sally Winterton
Debbi Young

Photograph Index

Recipe Index

THE *Bounty* OF
Chester County

HERITAGE EDITION

YOUR ORDER

	QTY	TOTAL
The Bounty of Chester County: Heritage Edition at $24.95 per book		$
Pennsylvania residents add $1.50 sales tax per book		$
Shipping and handling at $3.00 per book		$
TOTAL		$

Please make check payable to C.C.A.D.C.C.—*Heritage Edition.*

Name

Street Address

City   State   Zip

Telephone Number

To order by mail, send to:
Agricultural Development Council
Government Services Center, Suite 270
601 Westtown Road
West Chester, Pennsylvania 19380-0990

Photocopies will be accepted.